THE FOUNDER & THE FORCE MULTIPLIER

THE FOUNDER & THE FORCE MULTIPLIER

HOW ENTREPRENEURS AND EXECUTIVE ASSISTANTS ACHIEVE MORE TOGETHER

ADAM HERGENROTHER

WITH HALLIE WARNER

ADAM HERGENROTHER COMPANIES

THE FOUNDER & THE FORCE MULTIPLIER
How Entrepreneurs and Executive Assistants Achieve More Together

SECOND EDITION

ISBN   978-1-5445-3420-6   *Hardcover*

978-0-5784-3989-1   *Paperback*

978-1-5445-3616-3   *Ebook*

found·er
ˈfau̇n-dər

1. a person who starts their own company.
2. the beginner or originator of something.

force mul·ti·pli·er
/fôrs/ /ˈməltəˌplī(ə)r/

1. a strategic business partner who helps a leader build and run wildly successful businesses.
2. a leader's right-hand person.

CONTENTS

AN OPEN LETTER TO NEW AND RETURNING READERS

In 2019, we co-authored *The Founder & The Force Multiplier: How Entrepreneurs and Executive Assistants Achieve More Together.* When we wrote the book, our focus was on the partnership between an Entrepreneur and their right-hand employee (usually in the form of an Executive Assistant, Personal Assistant, or Chief of Staff). What we've realized over time is that the principles that we live by and value extend far beyond the scrappy early days of a startup, all the way to the C-suite of Fortune 100 companies. An effective strategic business partnership is a powerful thing—and yet it only works when both parties are committed to challenging each other and growing together every day.

What started with a blog became a book. And a book has turned into a movement. And that movement into an organization—The Founder & The Force Multiplier. The Founder & The Force Multiplier's mission is to help leaders and their Force Multipliers find their matches, strengthen their relationships, and become better leaders by providing coaching, training, consulting, technology, and other resources. Great, right?

But I know that what you *really* want to know is why we're publishing an updated version of the book. Well, it's been over three years since we published *The Founder & The Force Multiplier,* and a lot has changed. I received a strategic investment into one of our companies. We started building a technology solution for leaders and their right-hand strategic business partners. We started a podcast, launched Project | U, and started hosting Force Multiplier Cohorts. We swear much less (Well, at least I do. Hallie still has some work to do). We have navigated leading and growing multiple businesses during a global pandemic. We've grown as individuals and as leaders. Our partnership has evolved. We've shifted our perspective on a few issues. We've learned a lot, and we have more to share.

In this updated version, you'll find many of the same foundational concepts, with some of our new perspectives sprinkled in. As before, this book is best read together. Use it to start a conversation about how to be better strategic business partners and leaders for each other and your company. Together, you will both achieve more.

Need nothing and enjoy everything!

Adam   Hallie

PREFACE

FOUNDERS AND FORCE MULTIPLIERS

Your alarm goes off at 5:30 a.m. You hit snooze. It goes off again at 5:45 a.m. You jump out of bed, scrambling through your morning routine as you check emails while brushing your teeth, grab a protein bar as you slip on your suit jacket, and kiss your children on your way out the door as you're calling your first client of the day. You spot your wife in the upstairs window with the baby and give her a quick wave as you put your car into reverse. Half your brain is chatting with your client, and the other half is making a mental list of all the other calls, contracts, meetings, follow-ups, and projects you have to tackle that day. You're eleven months into your journey as a business owner, and every day feels like you're drowning. You're not present at home. You're not present with your clients. You're not present with your team. You're not giving your best to anyone or anything in your life. You're burning the candle at both ends, and you're on the brink of a breakdown. Something's got to give.

You need a Force Multiplier, a.k.a. an Executive Assistant, a strategic business partner who will bring order to the chaos and take on the miscellaneous 80 percent of your workload—and who will help you create the foundation that will allow you to build a life and business without limits.

* * *

Your alarm goes off at 5:30 a.m. You hit snooze. It goes off again at 5:45 a.m. You slowly get out of bed and pour yourself a cup of coffee, savoring each moment before you have to head to the office. You mindlessly scroll through your emails, opening the latest email from your boss, sighing, and rolling your eyes at his most recent ridiculous request. You debate calling in sick as you check LinkedIn for new job opportunities. You spend ten more minutes telling your husband how much you love your career as an Executive Assistant but currently feel trapped. You slip on your heels, grab another cup of coffee to go, and blast some early 2000s hip-hop on your way to the office to pump yourself up for the day ahead. You are already counting down the minutes until you can go home. You are uninspired, uninterested, and disengaged. You worry that it is starting to show in your work, and it's already affecting your personal relationships. Something's got to give.

You need a Founder, a.k.a. an Entrepreneur, a visionary, a driven and growth-minded leader who will reignite your passion for your career, challenge you to think bigger, and allow you to use your project management and leadership skills, along with your business acumen, to help him create the foundation that will allow you both to build a life and career without limits.

Does either of these situations sound familiar? Are you that Entrepreneur? Are you that Executive Assistant? An Entrepreneur and an Executive Assistant (EA) need each other to survive and thrive.

But it only works if you are working with the right strategic business partner.

BESIDE EVERY LEADER IS A TALENTED
FORCE MULTIPLIER. BESIDE EVERY FORCE
MULTIPLIER IS A VISIONARY LEADER.

If you are an Executive Assistant interested in learning how to build a dynamic and fulfilling career or a leader looking to hire or establish a better relationship with your right hand, then this book is for you. This book will explore the partnership between the Entrepreneur and the Executive Assistant. Read it together. Compare notes. Use it as a catalyst for engaging in fierce conversations. The power of the partnership only works when you are both committed to challenging each other and growing together every day.

PART ONE

THE FOUNDATION

- Confidence from Both leader / EA
- hearing from Both

1

-value of admin role

WHY YOU SHOULD LISTEN TO ANYTHING WE HAVE TO SAY

- Changing hats from friend to leader

Why should you listen to anything we have to say? Because we've gone through the ups and downs of an eleven-plus-year strategic partnership. Because entrepreneurship is in my blood and I have founded five successful organizations, and Hallie has been force multiplying by my side for a majority of that time. We don't have it all figured out. We're both far from perfect, and we've had our share of rough patches and growing pains over the past several years. But what I do know is that we are both committed to each other's success and the success of the companies. This is our story and what has worked for us. Every strategic partnership is a little different. It is our hope that the lessons you learn here will help you find success and fulfillment in your business and your career.

THE ORIGIN STORY

Ever since sixth grade, I've been a bit of a rebel. A few years ago, my mom found some old forms that I had her fill out for me (I already understood the power of delegation and leverage at a young age, even though I didn't know that was what it was.) One form asked what we wanted to be when we grew up and listed a series of options: Cowboy, Model, Astronaut…hell no. I wrote (okay, my mom wrote) Business Owner at the bottom. I really had no idea what that entailed, but I knew I had my own ideas and wanted to see them through. At twelve years old, I refused to have anyone put a limit on my thinking.

School was never my favorite place to be (and that is definitely an understatement). I started hanging out with the wrong crowd and dabbled in drugs, smoking cigarettes heavily, and using food as a way to numb my feelings and escape from just going through the motions of life. I hated the way I was living for a long time and in the process ended up more than one hundred pounds overweight, failing classes, and driving a piece-of-crap car. My self-worth was nonexistent. I was in a dark place and was completely unsatisfied with where my life was going. Enough was enough.

A BREAKING POINT

One day, when I was fifteen, I came home from school and just started crying. My dad found me like that in my room and said, "You have two choices. You can accept where you are, or you can change." There is that moment—you know the one—when you want to change, but nothing changes. And then you've had those other moments when you said, "This is it. No more." And in those moments, your life changes forever. You are fully committed to the new direction, and you cut ties, burn bridges, and leave behind the old you for good. That's what I did that day. I stopped caring what other people thought of me. I stopped hanging out with my old friends (who, it turns out, weren't really friends after all). Actually, these "friends" broke into my car and stole all of my belongings, which erupted into a series of fights over the next couple of weeks. My older brother had to come home from college with some of his friends; things got physical, and the police got involved. It was a total shit show. But I never backed down. I was committed to this new life. Eventually, they started bullying someone else.

I stopped letting other people dictate who I should be. From that moment on, I was determined to never let anyone put a limit on what I could do or who I could become. I was writing my own story.

THE TRANSFORMATION

A year after one of the lowest points in my life, I was one hundred pounds lighter—physically, mentally, and emotionally. I really started getting into sports at that point—hockey, snowboarding— and eventually settled on football. My junior year we won the state championship, and my senior year I was captain of the team along with a couple of other guys. What a difference those friends made, compared to the ones I was hanging out with before. Today, I am in business with two of those former football co-captains.

Despite how well I was doing on the football field, school and tests still weren't my thing. I wasn't good at taking tests, so my SAT scores sucked. Combine that with the fact that my grades my freshman year of high school were terrible. College was an option, but only in the guaranteed-admissions program at the University of Vermont (UVM), which meant that I had to get a 3.0 my first year of college to be fully accepted as a student there. Challenge accepted. There were five people from my high school who did the guaranteed-admissions program, but I was the only one to be accepted as a full-time student. I earned a 3.2 GPA my first year. I'm really proud of that because it was another example of the power of having clear vision and working harder than anyone else to get there.

During my freshman year at UVM, I had a friend who crashed on my couch but didn't actually go to school there. We all had one of those, right? He was selling cars and had this great opportunity for me to make a little extra money. We bought a car for $1,000—$500 cash in, each. It was all the money I had at the time (he was a good salesman!). My friend bought the car, fixed it up, and sold it a week or so later, and we doubled our money. What?! All I had to do was hand over some cash and do nothing else (I never even saw the car), and two weeks later my $500 turned into $1,000. It was the first time I had experienced leverage in the business world. But I would never have had that experience if I hadn't been willing to take the risk. No risk, no reward, right? Seemed like a pretty sweet deal to me, so I kept putting the money I made back into more car purchases with my buddy. After about six months and grossing about $40,000 each, he didn't need my capital contributions anymore and was going to move forward on his own.

I took my cash and bought a condo with my brother. It was a pre-construction unit (part of a large new condo complex) that we bought for $160,000: brand-new, spacious, great location. Once it was complete, we rented it out. Meanwhile, I was living in a basement. I'd seen success before with flipping cars, so I understood how important it was to put money into the business, or business deal, first. Personal comfort be damned! Everything was going fine until 2005, when our note was pulled and we were forced to sell (yeah, we weren't supposed to be renting the unit, and the bank found out). I thought it sucked to have to sell when everything in real estate was booming! But that peak meant we ended up being the highest sale in that development in almost ten years. Not a bad deal. I was starting to see how life could unfold *for* us, not simply happen *to* us.

BECOMING AN ENTREPRENEUR

When I graduated college, I started working as a commercial underwriter (which only lasted about six months before I was fired) and joined another company as a financial controller. The new job was great. I was a recent college graduate, and I had an assistant right away. I wasn't exactly sure how to navigate that relationship and often had her fetching me coffee, filing, and faxing documents for me. At the time, that was what I thought assistants did.

I was at that job for about a year and a half, but there were limits that came with working for someone else, at least at that organization. I needed to be free to think, explore, and experiment with my own ideas and my own business. I needed to be in control of my life.

Entrepreneurship and leverage are a part of who I am—from homework to cars to real estate. So in late 2006, I did what every sane person would *not* do during one of the biggest—if not *the* biggest—real estate bubbles in history: I quit my job, became a Realtor®, and started building a real estate team.

I quickly realized that if I wanted to achieve the levels of success I had envisioned, I would not be able to do it alone. When I began my career in real estate, I really started to understand the importance of leveraging to a great assistant. It wasn't just handing off miscellaneous tasks; it was creating a mutually beneficial relationship. I focused on sales, and my assistant focused on her strengths: handling marketing and client services and creating systems and processes to make my business run smoothly, which was good for business for both of us.

I had a lot of success quickly. Within my first couple of years in real estate, I was the Re/Max Associate of the Year and the Northwestern Vermont Board of Realtors Rookie of the Year. We had one of the top teams in New England, and I was named one of the nation's Top 30 Under 30 Realtors by *Realtor* magazine. The awards were great. People definitely knew who I was. But it wasn't enough. I wanted more freedom, more growth, and more opportunity for myself and for those I was in business with, so I decided to open up the first Keller Williams Realty office in Vermont.

FINDING MY FORCE MULTIPLIER

Over the next four years, as I was building my real estate team and later launching a real estate franchise, I went through several assistants, none lasting longer than eight months. It wasn't anyone's fault per se. I was relentlessly driven, incredibly fast-paced, and impatient, with an overall lack of leadership skills. The assistants I was hiring fell more in the reactive, rather than proactive, category. I didn't really understand how to properly hire talent back then, and I paid for it with high turnover—until 2010, when Hallie and I joined forces.

Hallie and I have been working together now for over eleven years. When we started working together, we were both in our mid- to late-twenties, hungry, and ready to just dominate the real estate and business world. I don't think Hallie quite knew what she was getting into, but she always figured it out. I initially hired her as a real estate marketing assistant in order to allow my current assistant to move into the Executive Assistant position. But within about three months I knew they were in the wrong roles. Hallie transitioned into the role as Executive Assistant, and the rest is history. By that time I owned a Keller Williams Realty Market Center and had a real estate team.

Fast-forward eleven years, and I still own the Keller Williams Vermont Market Center (number one office in the state) and Livian™ (a real estate company now in thirty-one locations around the country and counting). In addition, we've formed BlackRock Construction and Hergenrother Foundation, acquired two additional Keller Williams Market Centers, grown The Founder & The Force Multiplier, and launched Project | U (a yearlong, full-immersion leadership coaching program) and a podcast, *Business Meets Spirituality*. There have also been many other iterations and companies along the way. Hallie has been by my side in the business each step of the way, pissing me off by challenging my thinking, helping me set up or dissolve companies, hiring staff, keeping everyone on track, and supporting me in my personal and business life.

While Hallie is no longer my Executive Assistant (she replaced herself in that role in late 2017), she served as a combination of Chief of Staff, Executive Assistant, and Personal Assistant to me for over seven years.

Read on as Hallie shares how she came into my world.

HALLIE NARRATES: FINDING MY MATCH

Adam found me on Craigslist. Actually, I think one of his assistants at the time found me and called me in for an interview. I still remember the first day I met Adam. I was twenty-five years old and had just moved to the big city of Burlington, Vermont, from a very rural Vermont town. I was dressed to impress in my most professional business suit—all black (which is still my signature outfit) and purple suede heels for a pop of personality. Adam impressed me with his energy and direct, no-bullshit attitude. But even more than that, he had a vision to grow the business, and I could see that by aligning myself with him, I, too, would succeed.

I've been an "assistant" since I was fresh out of college, yet I always approached my roles as an emerging leader within the company. Whether it was my first professional job as a PR/marketing coordinator at a nonprofit or later as an Executive Assistant to the Principal at a public high school, I believed in leading and assisting. Yet it wasn't until I joined forces with Adam that I fully realized how I could harness my natural tendencies into a kick-ass career. A few days after I met Adam at his office, I was hired as a real estate marketing assistant, and I've been growing ever since. I may have honed my skills as an Executive Assistant while working with Adam, but more importantly, Adam taught me how to be a businesswoman and a leader.

HOW TO USE THIS BOOK TO MAXIMIZE YOUR RESULTS

Great! You're still here. Thanks for sticking around.

A big part of why we wrote this book is to show how important it is for Executives and Executive Assistants to find each other and then to teach them how to work together. You've made the commitment to invest your time and energy into creating a successful strategic business partnership, so we want to give you a few pointers about how to best use this book to maximize your results.

TITLES AND TERMS

Throughout this book, you will hear us use the terms Entrepreneur, Founder, Leader, and Executive. We may even throw in Business Owner and Boss from time to time. Those titles will encompass the CEO, business owner, Entrepreneur, VP, executive, etc., positions. Likewise, Executive Assistant will serve as an all-encompassing title for anyone fulfilling the role of Force Multiplier in your organization, regardless of title—Office Manager, Administrative Assistant, Executive Secretary, Chief of Staff, Director of Operations, etc.

If Force Multiplier is a new term to you, let me give you the lowdown. All of the "right-hand" positions above are Force Multipliers. Force multiplication refers to a factor or a combination of factors that dramatically increases (hence "multiplies") the effectiveness of an item or group, giving them the ability to accomplish greater things than would be possible without it. And that's just what Executive Assistants and Chiefs of Staff do.

In addition, we will generally be using "she" to reference the Executive Assistant position and "he" when referring to the Executive. This is our reality and does not serve to encompass all the gender and nonbinary pronouns potentially represented by Founders and Force Multipliers.

A NOTE ABOUT NARRATION

This book is broken into thirty-three chapters where you'll hear from both me and Hallie along the way. That's the power of the partnership. Two people, two halves of one great leader. I bring the vision, and Hallie follows through. We see each situation from different perspectives but are always aligned just enough to keep everything moving in the same direction, quickly and effectively. We're going to share what's worked for us, what we've learned along this journey, and some best practices that we recommend you implement immediately to get results. While I am narrating most of the book, you will hear from Hallie from time to time, which will be noted by "Hallie Narrates."

ACHIEVE MORE TOGETHER

At the end of most chapters, there will be a section called Achieve More Together. This will give leaders and their Force Multipliers the opportunity to reflect, engage in productive dialogue, and determine next steps to keep their partnership growing and thriving.

RESOURCES

You will also find a resource section at the end of the book. This will provide you with ways to connect with us and The Founder & The Force Multiplier community. In addition, we'll share links for you to tap into additional resources for further growth and leadership development.

All right, let's get started.

THE HISTORY OF THE ASSISTANT

When you hear the word "assistant," what comes to mind? Several decades ago, you may have thought of a *Mad Men* secretary fetching coffee, placing phone calls, and mixing midday cocktails. More recently, you may think of assistants as overworked and abused à la *The Devil Wears Prada*. But gone are the days of "office girls" and "gal Fridays." Today, assistants are in positions of power.

RIGHT-HAND MEN AND WOMEN

Assistants (previously known as secretaries) existed in Rome prior to the establishment of the empire. Theoretically, the secretary role emerged when prominent individuals needed confidential matters handled. Prior to the late 1880s, secretaries were usually men who spoke several languages and had a broad, generalized education. They were responsible for taking dictation, handling correspondence, maintaining account books, managing a growing amount of paperwork, and acting as trusted advisors. At the turn of the twentieth century, more and more women joined the workforce in clerical positions and began to implement new technology such as the telephone, typewriter, and adding machine. Throughout history, secretaries have played prominent (albeit often unacknowledged) roles in assisting heads of state, emperors, Entrepreneurs, presidents, and military leaders. What might our world look like today if these leaders hadn't had their right-hand people?

ASSISTING THE EXECUTIVE

In modern history, secretaries (later assistants) were brought into a company to take care of an Executive's day-to-day needs, as well as take notes and use office equipment that the Executive didn't have the time or inclination to figure out. While the role has definitely evolved over the years, some things remain the same. For example, most Executives don't want to be bothered with the minutiae of integrating Zoom with their Gmail, troubleshooting copier issues, or editing a Beautiful.ai presentation. Does that feel a little, well, entitled? Maybe, but that is not where their time is best spent. Hell, their time isn't even best spent putting the slide deck together. That's why they need a tech-savvy EA to translate their ideas and vision into a presentation that is clear, concise, and easily digestible by a diverse audience.

Founders and Force Multipliers are really responsible for one high-impact job; they simply make different contributions toward the overall goal. Regardless of what industry you are in, if you are an Executive, there are parts of your job that directly correlate to the bottom line. Think dollar-producing activities, such as lead generation, sales, talent acquisition and management, business development, sharing the vision, and leading the team. Other than those few tasks, everything else, 80 percent of your job, should be leveraged to someone else on your team. Sure, perhaps your marketing team or HR department handles some of this work, but they are not going to help you with your specific job. That's where an Executive Assistant comes in.

THE MODERN EXECUTIVE ASSISTANT

Your Executive Assistant will handle your 80 percent, while you focus on your top 20 percent of activities. Here's an example: you are in charge of leading the upcoming quarterly board meeting. It's your gig. No one else is going to do it for you—not marketing, not HR, not your sales team. However, over the next three months, you're traveling seven out of the twelve weeks, meeting with potential clients and speaking at a college alumni event, among the day-to-day tasks of leading your division. Enter your Executive Assistant. Your EA will ensure the venue is booked, AV is set up, the correct people are invited, an agenda is prepared and delivered, supporting documents are sent to stakeholders ahead of time, questions are answered, logistics are managed, water is poured, and lunch is catered. She will work with you to prepare (perhaps even write) your speech and will collect all relevant pieces of information from the correct parties to create a comprehensive presentation. You show up the day of the board meeting, and your EA hands you the presentation remote so you can do your thing.

Now, Executive Assistants weren't always this involved in the business. Often they were kept at a distance: answering phones, taking meeting minutes, making sure coffee and meals were procured, and managing the flow of paperwork through the office. Many assistants still handle those tasks and much, much more. EAs are critical staff and valuable members of the inner circle. Today's EAs are business-savvy leaders and are not content to sit on the sidelines. They want in on the action. They want to know that what they are doing is a value-add to their Executive and to the business as a whole. Because it is.

The new Executive Assistant is rewriting the history books.

WHAT'S IN A NAME?

When Hallie was twenty-three, she was offered a position as an Executive Secretary to the Principal of a public high school. It was a great career opportunity for her, and she accepted—with one condition. The title of the job would need to be changed to Executive Assistant (a more modern and accurate description of the role). They agreed. And thus began Hallie's life-long commitment to reframing and reforming job titles and descriptions.

The debate about job titles continues. One of the most frequent questions we get from our business contacts or through The Founder & The Force Multiplier network is about what someone should call their new hire. I tend to agree with Shakespeare: "What's in a name? That which we call a rose/By any other name would smell as sweet." Does it really matter what your title is? In the grand scheme of things, no. If you are providing value at a high level and getting results, then a title is irrelevant to the internal team. Some say it's simply semantics, while others believe a proper title clarifies the role and dispels confusion, especially in a large organization, and still others want clear titles because many have worked very hard to get promotions and, yes, to get the titles that come along with those increased responsibilities, seniority, and compensation.

From a business-owner and leadership perspective, I care most about getting results. In the early stages of our companies, I let many of my team members choose their titles. As we've grown, we've had to recalibrate. Here's where titles get tricky, especially for small companies or high-growth startups. Let's say you have a small team, and in order to solidify your company's reputation in the market (and let's be honest, stroke some egos) you've assigned your sole marketing assistant the title of Chief Marketing Officer (CMO). Sexy titles make everyone feel good, right? Sure, for a couple of years. When your company begins to grow, you may need to top-grade your marketing talent. Your CMO is fantastic but is not cut out to get your company through its next growth phase. You've determined you don't really need a CMO but rather a Director of Marketing (who is also less expensive), and your CMO is really a perfect fit for a Social Media Manager position. The ego that wanted the CMO title is bound to be hurt. It is going to feel like a demotion to that staff member when, in reality, they weren't really fulfilling the CMO role anyway.

I would caution leaders from assigning C-suite or even VP/Director titles when you're a small organization, unless you plan to stay small. If you do plan on growing, I would encourage you to think about being conservative with job titles so that your staff has somewhere to go and somewhere to grow, as well as allowing room to bring on other team members at various levels without disrupting the commitment and loyalty of some of your original staff. Clear titles can eliminate unnecessary internal conflict.

Now, back to the Executive Assistant position, specifically. That role (and the various titles that can accompany it) is its own complicated web.

Through our years of research on the Executive Assistant position, and from Hallie's networking with EAs from around the world, we both believe even more strongly that titles matter. Aside from the business perspective, there are several other reasons clearly defined roles, coupled with clear titles, are important. I think it is particularly important because the EA role is still largely misunderstood, and the more clarity we can provide to the public and various business sectors, the better. This affects promotions and compensation, internal and external communication, as well as future career growth. Here's why.

PROMOTIONS AND COMPENSATION

In April 2017, Hallie and I were invited to speak at a conference for Executive Assistants in Washington, DC. At the event, a Senior Executive Assistant brought up the topic of titles. She was proud of her accomplishments and had earned the right to the Senior Executive Assistant position. She was no longer an Executive Assistant, and she was adamant that the roles and titles be clearly defined. Hearing her explanation helped clarify things for me. This doesn't mean that the Senior EA is better than the EA, simply that their roles and responsibilities are different in her organization. They are both providing high value to their Execs. One may simply be supporting the chairman and overseeing a team of other admins, while the other is supporting two VPs, but I guarantee both have worked incredibly hard to get where they are.

Executive Assistants have to make sure their titles accurately reflect the responsibilities they have. This ensures fair compensation and allows the opportunity for growth. For example, if an individual is the first and only administrative professional at her company and is supporting an entire department yet is assigned the title of Chief Administrative Officer (at an administrative assistant salary), this could prove challenging when it comes time for a promotion (which often coincides with a compensation adjustment). Make sure your title reflects your responsibilities, and as your responsibilities change, adjust!

COMMUNICATION

We know that titles do not equate to power or authority, yet having a certain title does carry weight. Accurate titles provide clarity to both internal and external stakeholders. As the Executive Assistant to a prominent CEO, you may get further when making an out-of-the-box request. Conversely, in the real estate world that we are from, Executive Assistant, for many years, meant Director of Operations (thankfully, that is changing!). For years, Hallie has received requests from people around the country asking her for advice about their real estate team operations, but she hasn't served in that capacity in over eight years. They would need to speak to our Vice President of Operations. Again, clear titles enable clearer communication and help you get in touch with the right people to get what you want faster.

CAREER GROWTH

Titles are never as important as when you have decided to leave your organization for another opportunity. Let's say your title is Executive Assistant yet you are operating as an Operations Manager, and you are looking to move into a Director of Operations role. With the SEO optimization and keyword search used in today's recruiting processes, you would likely be overlooked for operations positions with the title of Executive Assistant. On the other hand, if your title is Director of Operations yet you serve the role of an Executive Assistant, on the surface, it doesn't always translate when you're interviewing for EA positions.

Clearly defined job descriptions are so important. For example, if you are functioning as an Operations Manager but your title is EA, you may not actually be qualified or have the skillset necessary to take on an EA position. Whether interviewing, posting your resume on job boards, attending networking events, or simply undergoing a quarterly review at your current company, make sure your title and job description accurately describe the work that you do to ensure appropriate compensation and future career opportunities.

HALLIE NARRATES: WHY MY TITLE IS CHIEF OF STAFF

Many people know me from my work with Adam at Keller Williams Realty Vermont and Livian, formerly Hergenrother Realty Group (two of the many organizations under the Adam Hergenrother Companies umbrella). Keller Williams Realty is one of the organizations that really gets the importance of an Executive Assistant and teaches Realtors to hire an assistant first when building their business. Smart move. A real estate Executive Assistant handles everything for a Realtor—marketing, client care, office management, transaction management, system creation, process implementation, and more.

As a real estate agent grows their business, the EA starts to leverage and will typically hire someone to handle marketing and someone to handle transactions, while the Executive Assistant supports the lead agent and helps oversee the team. A lot of people think this is what I do. But while Adam is a licensed Realtor, owns several real estate brokerages, and leads a national real estate company that operates in twenty-five states and counting, he hasn't actively participated in a real estate transaction in almost ten years (except for his personal real estate portfolio, of course). I haven't supported him in a real estate capacity in years, except for overseeing the administration for his personal properties.

As a relatively young organization, we are still in massive growth mode. About eight years ago, I needed leverage, and I began the search for an assistant. At the time, we split my role in such a way that the new hire would handle all email, travel, communication, scheduling, and other administrative tasks. We decided her title would be Executive Assistant, which meant I started a search for a new title (in a small office, two EAs to the CEO was too confusing). I did extensive research about the Chief of Staff role and Chief Operating Officer position and everything in between. I was looking to define both what I currently did and where I saw myself in ten, fifteen, thirty years. After much deliberation, I settled on Chief of Staff.

We had a few Executive Assistants over the course of a few years, but the individuals in that position ultimately didn't work out and I reabsorbed many of those tasks. By choice. I did leverage many other tasks (entire positions, in fact) to other staff members and new hires. As we continued to grow and evolve, our businesses reached a point, in mid-2017, where we needed to revisit the Executive Assistant hire. In October 2017, we brought on a new Executive Assistant, and I was able to fully move into the Chief of Staff position, which ultimately aligns with my strengths, passion, and career goals.

In fact, at the end of 2017, I was so relieved that we had found a capable Executive Assistant that I decided it was time for me to leave the organization and try something new. That lasted just under a month before I was back in Adam's office having one of our famous fierce conversations. What did I want? What were my strengths? Where was I going? What did Adam need? What was next? After almost three hours and various ideas of where I could best contribute to the organization, I concluded the same thing that I did years before: I am meant to be a Chief of Staff. I am fortunate that Adam has allowed me to create such a dynamic and fulfilling career for myself.

WHICH ROLE IS THE RIGHT ONE?

So who do you hire? Executive Assistants wear so many different hats, and the role is incredibly diverse depending on the Executive, the company, and the industry. Executives must understand who they are looking for once they decide to hire an "assistant." Is the Executive looking for a Chief of Staff or a Personal Assistant, a COO or an Executive Assistant? Different titles and job descriptions will attract different types of talent. Executives, make sure you have the right person on your team based on your current and future needs. Executive Assistants, make sure you are in the right role, or perhaps take a look at other similar positions that may be a better fit. Of course, depending on the size of the organization, an Executive Assistant may be fulfilling all of these roles. However, as an organization or Executive grows or as the EA moves on to different career opportunities, the positions do, in fact, exist in isolation.

FORCE MULTIPLIER POSITIONS

Again, clarity is power for career satisfaction and a successful long-term partnership. Let's break down the most common positions that often end up with the title of Executive Assistant.

virtual admin is the same
in person - maybe an[?] at desk

Personal Assistant: A Personal Assistant manages the personal and family life of an Executive. This position can overlap with the Executive Assistant. The Personal Assistant and Executive Assistant work together to manage the Executive's schedule. The Personal Assistant is responsible for personal items such as personal bills, household purchases, family travel, medical appointments, and personal events.

Administrative Assistant: An Administrative Assistant assists with the day-to-day administrative details for an office, a division, or multiple Executives. Most Administrative Assistant duties revolve around creating order, managing and distributing information within the office, supporting productivity, and solving logistical issues. This may include such tasks as managing the flow of internal and external communication, arranging meetings and travel, greeting clients and customers, managing files, performing tech support, maintaining physical and electronic files, managing the office, and marketing.

Operations Manager: An Operations Manager is responsible for establishing internal and external processes, creating and maintaining systems, and setting key performance indicators for the business. She ensures that the company has the proper operational controls and administrative reporting procedures to meet operational and financial targets.

Executive Assistant: An Executive Assistant is a tactical genius and is responsible for managing the Executive. Executive Assistants live in the now…or usually one week to thirty days out. This doesn't mean that they aren't planning for future events or travel or chipping away at longer-term projects. It simply means their work is driven by the demands of the day and week—meeting prep; handling phone calls, emails, and visitors; scheduling; answering questions that come into the Executive Office; keeping the CEO on track and on time; managing and organizing files and information; researching; preparing travel; etc. In addition, the Executive Assistant maximizes the CEO's reach through her exceptional leadership and communication skills.

Chief of Staff: A Chief of Staff is a high-visibility strategic partner who supports her leader with effective decision-making, project management, and execution of strategic initiatives across all departments or companies. The Chief of Staff lives in the future...or a minimum of ninety days out (anywhere between ninety days and one year, and often beyond). She handles what she must in the moment, but much of her time is focused on long-term planning and projects to ensure the growth of the organization and the success of the leader. Her work is driven by the demands of the leader's long-term vision—interviewing for future leadership positions, creating a family office, writing a book, creating presentations or speeches to share the vision, meeting with potential business partners, refining recruiting and retention processes, establishing OKRs (objectives and key results), and more.

Recently, we've seen some other titles gain prominence, including Administrative Business Partner, Executive Business Partner, and Executive Support Professional.

Remember, all of the positions above are Force Multipliers. They are the right hand to a busy Executive who will ensure the implementation of their vision in various ways. Who are you? Who do you want to become? Who do you need in your life to help you get there?

Now that we all have a little clarity, let's dive into the most important aspects of a leader and a Force Multiplier's role and how they each contribute to the success of the organization.

ACHIEVE MORE TOGETHER

- Which Force Multiplier position do you need to hire first or next to help grow your business?
- Which title most accurately reflects your current Force Multiplier? Is a change needed?
- Write a job description for the Force Multiplier you need to hire.
- Force Multipliers, which role are you currently fulfilling? Do your job title, job description, and compensation accurately reflect your responsibilities?
- Executive Assistants, what is your next opportunity for growth? Does that job currently exist in your organization, or can you create it?
- Review your resume. Ensure your title, responsibilities, and contributions are accurate and up to date.
- If needed, schedule a time for a career and compensation conversation with your Executive.

THE TOP 20 PERCENT FOR LEADERS AND FORCE MULTIPLIERS

We know that for Entrepreneurs and Executive Assistants, the responsibilities are pretty much endless. It doesn't matter if you are a two-person team or if you are responsible for a team of two thousand people spread out around the globe. The days are long and the to-do lists even longer. Even if you never added one more task or new idea to your list, I bet you would have years of work still left to accomplish. This is why it is so important to have the top 20 percent of your job at the forefront of your mind at all times. I would even argue that the 20 percent for the EA and the Executive are the same. The only difference is who is doing what part of the job. An EA is there to help the Executive complete his work. It's like taking one massive job and splitting it down the middle based on each of your strengths.

REMEMBER THE 80/20 RULE

Let's do a quick refresher on the 80/20 Rule (Pareto Principle). The 80/20 Rule says that 20 percent of your input produces 80 percent of your results. So it is incredibly important to choose your 20 percent wisely. Everything does not matter equally. The Executive and EA must be on the same page to make sure they are executing on the same most important tasks. Typically, the 20 percent encompasses projects or responsibilities that the Executive is uniquely positioned to handle that move the financial meter of the business forward.

The EA is responsible both for making sure she helps her Executive complete his 20 percent as well as making sure the Executive doesn't become distracted with the miscellaneous 80 percent. Basically, an EA has to focus 100 percent on 100 percent of the job. It's a tall order, which is why a true EA business partner is hard to find. For EAs, this is where leading up will come into play. It is also imperative that the Executive and EA meet regularly in order to set the priorities for the week, month, or quarter so that each can execute on those high-priority items.

IDENTIFY THE LEADER'S 20 PERCENT

Too many Executives are still stuck in their email or managing their own calendars, scheduling and rescheduling meetings. That is not the best use of their time. That is certainly not their 20 percent. Now, identifying a leader's top 20 percent is relatively subjective—is he the director of a division, the Founder of an organization, a serial Entrepreneur, or a CEO of a Fortune 500 company? Regardless, most leaders' time is best spent on new business development, strategy, coaching and leading their senior staff, communicating and reinforcing the vision, setting the direction of the organization, and making quality decisions every day.

At some point in your entrepreneurial journey, you're going to wake up and realize that you no longer have a job. Okay, that could be because you built up your company and sold it, but more often than not, it's because you have surrounded yourself with great talent and you are no longer needed in the day-to-day operations of your company. You might be bored or feel inadequate, or you might start causing problems in your business just to have problems to fix. (I'm not the only one who does that, right?) Sure, you may not be working in the business any longer, but it is still your "job" to lead the organization. You are no longer doing the financials, making sales calls, interviewing, writing contracts, etc. So you show up to the office and do what? You lead.

There are three core components that make up a leader's 20 percent. Let's break them down.

1. CAST THE VISION

Sharing the vision with your team and with the public cannot happen often enough. It is your job to spread the vision through every conversation, in every interaction with the media, and through social media, marketing, and branding. Teaching and training is one of the best ways to spread the vision to a wide audience. Some people will love it (and you), and some people will hate it. But by sharing the vision, you will attract the people who should be in your life and who will help you grow your business. As a leader, casting the vision wide and often is your job.

2. PROVIDE FOCUS, CLARITY, AND DIRECTION FOR THE TEAM

All right, you've shared the vision—five, ten, or twenty years out. You've attracted talent who want to be on the journey with you, and they see the vision…vaguely. They are excited about it but don't quite understand how to get there or how they are going to contribute. It's your job to provide extreme clarity and focus on exactly what needs to be done that day, that week, that month, to drive the entire organization forward. Cultivate a culture where asking great questions is the norm and where you allow your team to push you and challenge your thinking. The vision might be crystal clear in your mind, but you've got to slow down long enough to explain your vision so that your team can put it into action.

Then take it a step further. There are going to be stretches of weeks and months when nothing seems to be going right. This is when you really need to double down and keep your people on track. Get them to focus on one thing they could do to make a significant impact that day. Sometimes this means telling them to set aside a smaller project and extending a deadline to focus all their time and attention on another priority. But tell them. Otherwise, they are trying to do it all and getting nothing done. For a leader, setting the direction and keeping your team focused is your job.

3. MAKE QUALITY DECISIONS

Once your team understands the vision and is focused on the most important ways they can individually contribute to the company's goals, then it's your job to make the best decisions for the good of the team and the company. On average, we each make 35,000 decisions per day. The best leaders focus on learning how to make world-class decisions. Remember, billionaires are not at all special, gifted, or uniquely positioned for success—they just have the clarity to make decisions that compound the growth of their organizations. For a leader, making quality decisions every day that propel your business forward is your job.

Maybe it goes without saying, but all of the above would not be possible if you were not constantly working on yourself and your personal and professional development and increasing your leadership lid. You will not be able to serve others or be the leader you need to be if your own tank isn't full. Read, journal, exercise, meditate, attend conferences, teach. Do whatever you need to do in order to grow and to keep making your world bigger so that your team and others continue to see you as a vehicle for their success.

This may seem like an oversimplification; however, I didn't say these were the *only* things a leader must do. I said that they were the most important. As I mentioned before, at some point your job will simply be to read or to think, but make sure you are sharing what you read and learn with others. Cast the vision; provide focus, clarity, and direction; and make quality decisions. That is your job as a leader. And in order to do it at the highest level possible, you're going to need some help.

Enter the Executive Assistant. The Executive Assistant role is one of the least-understood positions, in part because it encompasses so many different responsibilities and can differ greatly depending on the industry or the Executive/Entrepreneur. Here's Hallie to break down how an Executive Assistant force multiplies her leader's 20 percent.

HALLIE NARRATES: HOW AN EXECUTIVE ASSISTANT FORCE MULTIPLIES HER LEADER'S 20 PERCENT

The Executive Assistant position is complex and still largely misunderstood. My husband doesn't even fully understand what I do (and I talk about my work a lot). So what does an Executive Assistant do? Whatever it takes.

In the past five years or so, I have seen significant improvements in both the perception of the position and the training available for this career. Yes, executive support is a career. I was happy to discover that it was actually very fulfilling and lucrative because it was made for me (a type A, over-achieving, organized, detail-oriented, intrapreneurial leader).

Executive Assistants are the ultimate Force Multipliers and project managers. Their project just happens to be their Executive. From purchasing unique gifts for a business associate to managing internal and external communication, preparing speeches, reorganizing staff roles, creating business plans, and everything in between, they've got it covered. Executive Assistants are problem-solvers and fixers. They are some of the most resourceful and connected individuals in your organization. If you have a challenge, bring it to your nearest EA, and I guarantee she will have a solution for you by the end of the day. Executive Assistants are leaders, and seeing them as anything else is a complete underestimation of their ability and a disservice to the Executive and the company.

The Executive Assistant position is even more unique when you're talking about working with a Founder, Entrepreneur, or public figure. In April 2018, I attended a retreat just outside of Seattle where Monique Helstrom, former Chief of Simon Sinek, and current Speaker, Activator, and Unlocker of Human Potential, was a guest speaker. She was explaining a bit about her position and told us that she was recently talking to another assistant who works for a prominent thought leader/public speaker. While in theory they are in the same position—EAs to very prominent thought leaders, authors, and public speakers—Monique said their roles were completely different. I think that is a perfect illustration of why the role is so hard to define in any real specifics. The Executive Assistant position varies so significantly depending on what industry you work in, how established the organization is, and the personality and behavior of your Executive.

As Adam mentioned previously, a leader's 20 percent is casting the vision, establishing clear direction and focus, and making quality decisions. Clear and concise. Well, what about an Executive Assistant's 20 percent? It tends to get a bit murky, but I think this sums it up:

> An Executive Assistant's 20 percent is ensuring the objectives, goals, and vision of the Executive are organized, communicated, delegated, and executed.

I have been the Executive Assistant, and now Chief of Staff, for over eleven years with the same Executive, yet my job today looks nothing like it did on day one. The only constant is that I am still responsible for, and committed to, ensuring that Adam's vision is implemented.

Let's take that fairly abstract idea and put it into practice. In theory, the Executive Assistant's 20 percent is the Entrepreneur's bottom 80 percent, right? She handles all the miscellaneous tasks and administrative responsibilities, allowing the Executive to stay focused on leadership, strategy, business development, and communication. But we all know EAs aren't just going to focus on the 80 percent; part of their job is helping their Executive manage his 20 percent. Like Adam said, an EA focuses 100 percent on 100 percent of the job.

The 0–10 Principle

Adam has a really great analogy for this concept that I like to call the 0–10 Principle. As a visionary, Adam has brilliant ideas on the daily. They may not be completely fleshed out, but he has the spark and then sees the end result crystal clear. It is my responsibility to take that idea from about a 1 or a 2 to a 9 and then bring it back to him so he can do his final finessing to bring it to a 10. Here's what that looks like in practice. Adam wants to create an inspirational speaker series that raises funds for his foundation. Great! That's at about a 2. I will then take that idea, gather the necessary people, create a timeline and budget, put together a marketing plan, interview speakers, plan the event, and come back to Adam with a final plan, including the speaker lineup. He will offer additional insight, perhaps tweak the speaker order, and come up with an overarching theme for the night. Now we've got a 10. Executive Assistants, remember, this doesn't mean that you have to be the one to implement all of the pieces. Use your resources, staff, and leadership skills to work through others to get the project done.

That is how Executive Assistants help their leaders with their 20 percent. You can apply the concept to almost every aspect of your Executive's 20 percent, from drafting a letter to include in the company's annual report to revamping his blog, to preparing for a quarterly off-site leadership meeting to planning a fortieth birthday trip for his brother. An Executive Assistant manages the people, details, timelines, etc., to make an idea come to life. This can happen on a large scale, like helping him write a book, or on a smaller scale, like choosing the perfect anniversary gift for his wife. Let's break this down even further and look at how an EA helps the Executive with his 20 percent.

Force Multiply the Vision

Communicating the vision is perhaps the most critical component of an Executive's job. Casting the vision wide and often through strategic thought leadership initiatives generates new business, attracts talent, and boosts employee engagement. Thought leadership and casting the vision go hand in hand.

Executive Assistants can force multiply the vision by scheduling regular company updates. These can be in the form of town halls, a letter from the CEO in the annual report, daily blog posts, quarterly video announcements, weekly emails, monthly company meetings, etc. What matters here is that there is a cadence to the communication and that the leader is casting the vision and keeping the team updated and informed regularly. It is the EA's responsibility to schedule these, make sure the cadence is kept, and draft these letters, video scripts, newsletters, and so forth. Make sure the CEO's vision is heard often!

In addition, along with the marketing or brand-strategy teams, an EA must review the Executive's social media regularly to ensure that the messaging is in line with the company's mission and the Executive's vision. Once the brand is established, the EA must protect it and ensure that the messaging is consistent across all channels. How your Executive shows up at church needs to be the same way he shows up on YouTube.

EAs are in a unique position to pitch their Executives for interviews on blogs, national media publications, podcasts, radio shows, etc. They know their Executive's story. They know his language and how he would answer questions. Submit the Executive for awards and for as many media mentions as makes sense. The EA can craft the message that the Exec wants heard, and usually these initial media mentions lead to even bigger opportunities. Don't be afraid to start small and build up the brand presence. It all serves to ensure your leader's vision is heard.

The EA can also help the Executive write a weekly blog or host a weekly LinkedIn Live. The key is consistently creating opportunities for your Executive to deliver the vision for the organization and help position him as a thought leader in his industry.

Force Multiply Communication

Casting the vision means communication with both internal and external stakeholders, so how can an EA enhance these activities to maximize her leader's reach?

First, the EA can and should listen on calls and participate in meetings to make note of anything that the Executive says will be done, delivered, or followed up on. Does the Executive say he'll make an introduction or get the name of a book to someone? It is the EA's job to ensure that promises made are promises kept.

Managing internal and external relationships is critical. The EA can also force multiply a leader's communication by maintaining a database that houses important, and sometimes seemingly irrelevant, information about people. This can be family members, employees, candidates, vendors, community members, former employees, competitors, business leaders, etc. As the EA and Executive meet with people and conduct research or meeting prep, store any details about the meeting or the individual. Set reminders for anniversaries, birthdays, or important life milestones. I recommend using an inexpensive customer relationship management (CRM) system so you can set tasks and follow-up reminders so you don't miss an important date. Create a VIP list of people with whom the Executive wants to either maintain or create relationships. Then set up Google alerts that keep you in tune with what these people are doing, awards their companies receive, etc. It's a perfect opportunity for the Executive Assistant to remind the Executive to reach out, call, email, or send a handwritten note. The Executive will run into these players at conferences or networking and social events. Keep this information handy so you can pull it out and give it to the Executive as a quick refresher before he goes to a community event and forgets to congratulate a potential business partner on their recent merger.

Don't forget, the art of the handwritten note is not dead! Incorporate handwritten notes into the correspondence with the Executive's VIP list. It could be one of the most impactful ways to maximize the Executive's reach and build relationships. Whether that is thanking someone for coming in to meet with the Executive or congratulating a competitor on building a new office, handwritten notes get noticed. Pop a business card in there (because not everyone can interpret the Executive's handwriting and signature like the EA can). To really maximize the company's reach, the EA should write thank-yous and general notes to vendors or, for example, to the concierge who went above and beyond to help book a massage for the Executive when he arrived at their hotel. The more relationships that the EA can form, the better; this will only help her help the Executive. You never know when a kind word or just knowing the name of the right person at a restaurant will come in handy. Provide value, expecting nothing in return, and it will be returned tenfold.

If the EA travels with the Executive for speaking engagements or if she hosts training events where the Executive is the keynote presenter, she must pay attention to the audience. This is a great way to ensure she is maximizing her leader's communication. What content is resonating? What content could be removed for the next training event? After the event, he can update and refresh his content accordingly. EAs are the eyes and ears while Executives are presenting. Watch the room. Who is fully engaged and asking questions? Who is leaving the room every five minutes? Is there talent in the room? After the presentation (especially if it is a daylong event), the Executive is going to be fried and may need to catch a flight home, yet everyone is going to want to talk to him. Often, the Executive will have a line of people who want to thank him or ask questions. The EA should position herself next to the Executive to take business cards, take notes on who to follow up with, answer questions, or take photos. And, perhaps most importantly, to grab the Executive and steer him toward the exit so he doesn't miss his Uber!

Force Multiply Focus, Clarity, and Direction

For the Executive Assistant, force multiplying focus, clarity, and direction is all about leading and managing up so the Executive is making the right decisions, has the right meetings on his calendar, and is in relationships with the right people in order to achieve the company's objectives. If one of the Executive's primary goals is to ensure the team is on track and to focus on what must be done that day, week, or month, then that's the Executive Assistant's goal too.

To help your leader with the focus, clarity, and direction of the organization, when scheduling or drafting regular communication for him, make sure the message is clear and ties back into specific tasks that keep everyone focused.

Furthermore, during key leadership meetings, note all action items, and follow up accordingly. If there are no clear action items, do not leave the meeting without everyone agreeing on what the next best steps are or what the course of action is and who is accountable for what activities. Didn't catch it in the meeting? Make sure you follow up with each stakeholder and communicate the action plan to everyone by the end of the day.

Perhaps most importantly, when the Executive is getting hit from multiple angles or when he starts chasing a shiny object, it's the EA's duty to remind him of what is important and what the team has agreed to focus on that week, month, or quarter. Entrepreneurs are visionaries and have endless ideas. Make note of them, and if they aren't part of the overall goals, table them for now. If the Executive asks about them twice, then it's time to bring them to the forefront and get his buy-in that they should be moved to the top of the list—which may mean that another project will have to be tabled for the time being.

Force Multiply Making Quality Decisions

Once the vision is cast and everyone is clear on what they need to focus on for success, help your Executive make quality decisions day in and day out to keep the company growing and thriving.

For example, research tools and provide cost-benefit analysis to your Executive so he can make the best decision for the team. In addition, make sure the Executive is regularly available for impromptu meetings. While you may be the gatekeeper, do not block access to the "throne." Schedule time for the Executive to walk around and check in with people. Do not overschedule him so much that he's not available for a decision-making meeting that, if left undecided, could hold up a project for days.

Finally, be the eyes and ears for the Executive. Bring him the challenges (and solutions) of issues that, if not nipped in the bud, could fester and create organizational issues. Information is power, and it's important to bring the right information to your Executive so that he can have necessary context to make critical decisions for the company. This could be employee morale, inefficiencies in staffing, or a clunky system. Speak up, and help find a solution so your Executive can make a quality decision and everyone can keep moving forward.

Remember, the Executive's 20 percent is also the Executive Assistant's 20 percent. They may complete different tasks to get there, but they are both part of making it happen.

Now, back to Adam.

opportunity to weigh for –

PART TWO

THE STRATEGIC
PARTNERSHIP

THE STRATEGIC PARTNERSHIP

Now that the foundation is set, let's talk about how Founders and Force Multipliers build a strategic partnership. Neither party will be able to achieve their full potential without it.

While the term "strategic partnership" is a bit overused at this point, I'm not going to help the situation. In the case of the Executive and Executive Assistant, there isn't a more accurate term to describe the relationship, except perhaps "C-suite symbiosis." A strategic partnership is a mutually beneficial relationship with both parties working toward a common goal, and that's just what Executive Assistants and leaders do.

BRINGING OUR STRENGTHS

While EAs are technically in a support role, the more the Executive and EA can approach their working relationship as a partnership, the better. Executives can't do their jobs without Executive Assistants, and Executive Assistants wouldn't be able to do their jobs without Executives. The ideal strategic partnership is a business relationship where each party is dedicating their time and resources to the partnership, rooted in their strengths. Each party is accountable for their contribution and deliverables.

In a strategic partnership, there is exceptionally clear and consistent communication, as well as mutual respect and trust. In short, when we talk about the Founder and Force Multiplier or the Entrepreneur and Executive Assistant, we're talking about one role, one job, that takes two people, focused on their strengths, to get it done.

SURVIVING PARTNERSHIP CHALLENGES

Several years ago, my strategic partnership with Hallie was put to the test when we had a very real, very fierce conversation (the first of many!). Hallie needed her next growth opportunity and was not sure if her needs could be fulfilled with me and at our company. That conversation made me examine myself as a leader and provided me with my own growth opportunity. That conversation was also a testament to the trust and loyalty we had established over the previous five-plus years of working together. Many people would have been looking for jobs for three months and then would have started the conversation by giving their two weeks' notice. Hallie did not want to leave my organization, and I didn't want her to either. But things needed to change. So we discussed those issues and began working on a ninety-day plan to get her into her strength zone. She has dedicated the past eleven years to me and my vision, and in turn, I have dedicated myself to continually increasing my leadership lid for her and all of my team members. That is a strategic partnership.

Hallie pisses me off almost daily, but that is a good thing. If you don't have someone you trust who is challenging your thinking and pushing you to be a better leader, then it's probably not the right relationship. While she supports me daily, I don't think of her as an "assistant," but rather as a business partner. Whatever projects I'm working on or decisions I'm making for the organization, she is privy to and part of the process. She maximizes my time and maximizes my reach by acting as an extension of me at all times. When she speaks, she is speaking on my behalf, and I trust her to do so. Now, this didn't happen overnight. We've both made mistakes (a lot of them), made many conscious sacrifices, and learned a lot over the past decade, but we have done it together.

CREATING A STRATEGIC PARTNERSHIP

I'm a man of action, so how do we put the theory of the strategic partnership into practice? There are five key things you can do to create a strategic partnership with your Executive Assistant:

1. Give up control.
2. Meet and communicate regularly.
3. Set clear expectations, goals, and wins.
4. Build trust.
5. Invite her into the inner circle.

Throughout the rest of this section, we will explore how Entrepreneurs and Executive Assistants can create true business partnerships. We'll share with you what has worked for us in the hopes that you can take some of our strategies and experiences and apply them to your partnership. Every partnership is unique. It's the commitment to learn, work, and grow together that ultimately determines whether or not you create a successful partnership.

HOW TO GET YOUR BOSS TO GIVE UP CONTROL

Entrepreneurs and Executive Assistants must work side by side in order to maximize the partnership and get more done. Note that I said side by side. While we've established that the Executive and the EA are essentially handling one very big role with endless responsibilities, they are not doing the same activities to accomplish their shared goals. This means you each must stay in your own lane and let the other person do their own thing. Executives, you must give up control in order to allow your EAs to shine. Believe me, you definitely cannot do it better than a great Executive Assistant.

A great EA will help you delegate and will pull work away from you (and not let you have it back). A talented EA will not tolerate being micromanaged and, in fact, will end up leading you to a certain degree. If you don't give up control over every email, every meeting, every marketing piece, etc., then either you *are* the assistant and should not have made a hire in the first place, or

stant will leave and find an Executive who will allow her
: job and do it well!

You'll never see someone's full potential or allow them to grow if
you don't give up control. Before you know it, things will just be
handled and often you won't even have known you needed them
done! Giving up control gives you the space to focus on *your* 20
percent, not your EA's. However, this is easier said than done.

One of the most common questions we get from Executive Assistants around the world is, "How do I get my boss to give up
control?" Conversely, I also get asked by leaders, "Why should
I hire an EA? What would she even do? Do I have enough work
for her? How do I lead her?" Clearly, there needs to be some give
and take. It's a partnership, after all!

We know Executives hire EAs for a reason, so why are they doing
half of the EA's job? I believe it is an integral part of the Executive
Assistant's job to communicate with the Executive how best to
work with her, while showcasing her own talents, going above and
beyond to deliver, and building trust in order to take on even more.

When your Executive is in extreme micromanagement mode,
acting particularly controlling, or exhibiting this as a new behavior,
you must come from a place of curiosity, not judgment. I always
like to start with the simple question "Why?" Above all, do not
dismiss it simply as "That is just the way he is." That may be true.
That may, in fact, be his natural behavioral style, but if you want
to be a leader and a strategic partner, you must learn how to navigate this behavior, communicate accordingly, and get stuff done.
If nothing else, it will create a much more fulfilling and pleasant
work environment for you.

So why is your boss a control freak? Get curious. What is going on at home, in his personal life, or even within the company that might be causing him more stress than usual? Is he feeling out of control in a certain area of his life (perhaps with a sick relative, an unhealthy lifestyle, or an unhappy marriage)? In order to feel in control amid other chaos, he may be doubling down and controlling whatever he can, which may mean you and your work.

To a certain degree, being seen as an ally in the C-suite comes with time. You can help move this process along by helping your Executive give up control. Here's how.

WATCH FOR TRIGGERS

Keep an eye out for various triggers. Does he get particularly controlling when he is about to meet with the Chairman of the Board or when he is presenting the quarterly financials to the company? Perhaps he made a big mistake on a previous project and now every time a similar project comes across his desk, he holds on even tighter to every detail. Notice the patterns, and then you can begin to anticipate this behavior and take action to mitigate stress for both you and your Executive. Whether you start to overcommunicate, prepare to spend longer days at the office, or simply add in one or two extra yoga classes (for you) leading up to a big presentation, the key is to identify the triggers and plan accordingly. Bonus points for pointing this out to your Executive and coming up with a plan together to work through these stressful times.

When Hallie and I first began working together, my schedule was one of my triggers. I didn't want anyone managing my schedule because I felt like they were taking away my options, which to me meant taking away my freedom. I am fueled by freedom, so I didn't want anyone telling me what to do or where to be. This was a process we had to work through together. Hallie needed me to have more structure and predictability in my day in order to maximize my time and effectiveness. We discussed options and eventually blocked my calendar off for two hours in the middle of the day where I have completely unscheduled time to walk around the office, check emails, check in with our leadership team, eat lunch, meditate, or just leave! The morning and afternoon blocks were then free for Hallie to schedule me however she felt would best serve the needs of our growing organization. Because we meet regularly to discuss priorities, ensuring that my days remain strategic and that I'm only spending time on those things that matter most, Hallie and my EA are able to plan accordingly. Giving up control of my calendar made us all more purposeful.

TRAIN YOUR EXECUTIVE

Your Executive may never have worked with an Executive Assistant before. What you perceive to be control-freak behavior may simply be his lack of knowing any better! Or maybe his previous EA was an order-taker, not the initiative-taking badass that you are. In this case, it's your responsibility to show your Executive how to work best with you. What if you are a master at website design and your Executive has no idea? Meanwhile, he's been wanting to start a blog to attract more talent to the organization. It's your responsibility to share your strengths and see where those can fit into your Executive's needs. It's up to you to develop your career. Part of that may be having a conversation with your Executive to let him know that you feel you are being underutilized and that you bring (insert your talent) to the table and can contribute more in specific ways to benefit your Executive and the company.

ASK FOR FORGIVENESS

On occasion, it is better to ask for forgiveness rather than asking for permission. Depending on what the task is and how risk-tolerant you are, take a go at it, and then immediately ask for feedback—if it's something you know you can handle and if it has minimal impact on the organization, that is. For example, booking dinner reservations that you know you can cancel, ordering much-needed office equipment that you know you can return, or returning all of your Executive's voicemails to either provide the correct information or get additional information for your Exec to review. Just communicate what you did and get that feedback so you can adjust next time if needed.

HANDLING A NEW EXECUTIVE

If an Executive is new to the position, he could be feeling insecure about his new role and reverting to comfortable behavior. A coaching client recently told Hallie that her boss moved from Chief of Staff to CEO and was still handling all her own email communication (not necessarily the best use of her time). Stakeholders were loving the personal attention they were getting from the Chief of Staff-turned-CEO, and the CEO had now set a precedent where hearing from the "assistant" felt like a slight. This situation calls for some extreme leading up. This new Executive was likely sticking to what she knew and what she was comfortable with, as well as enjoying the fact that she was gaining a certain amount of significance by wowing her stakeholders with her responsiveness. In this case, you will need to remind the Executive that you can handle the communication and help her move into the new responsibilities of her role. She will still want to feel valued, so find ways for her to contribute to or personally communicate with her team or investors, such as weekly lunches, handwritten notes, and surprise-and-delight moments for the team.

UNDERSTAND MICROMANAGING

Why do Executives micromanage? It could be one of several reasons.

Some Executives use micromanaging as a distraction. They would rather be checking in with you or various team members instead of sitting down to accomplish a difficult project or have a tough conversation. Other Entrepreneurs and Executives have worked for years to build a business or to climb the corporate ladder. They micromanage because the business, the company, or their career is their baby. It is especially hard for them to give up control because often they did everything on their own for many years. Or they're cognizant that if something fails, not only are their income and livelihood at stake, but so are the jobs of many, many people.

Finally, controlling bosses may also just be trying to help! The book *Multipliers: How the Best Leaders Make Everyone Smarter,* by Liz Wiseman, talks about the "accidental diminisher," the leader who is so helpful and always swooping in to save the day before staff members can figure things out for themselves or make mistakes. This kind of leader means well, but this behavior, too, comes from fear. Even as well intentioned as it is, this micromanaging only hinders the growth of the individual and the organization.

Do any of these sound familiar? Once you've identified the root cause of the controlling behavior, you can put an action plan in place to combat the controlling tendencies and build trust. A lot of it is going to come down to having a conversation with your Executive about your working relationship. You will need to voice your strengths, show and tell (don't ask) how you can assist, and iterate the benefits of you taking over certain tasks and projects.

SHOW HIM THE MONEY

The most common areas where an Executive may be unwilling to give up control involve email and scheduling (which should be the very first to go!). This is where you must show him the money. Let's say he is spending two hours a day managing his email and calendar. What dollar-producing activity could he be doing during those two hours instead? He could recruit a top-producing sales professional who brings over their book of business, or he could put together a training seminar that brings in thousands of dollars, attracts talent, and builds the company's brand. Bring him the data and facts, and make your case. His time is best spent on growth, not on operational and administrative activities—that's your job!

GIVE IT A TRIAL PERIOD

If all else fails, give the trial period approach a try. For example, if you want to take over email communication for your Executive, ask if you can try managing his email for the next two weeks—and if it doesn't work out, he can have his email back. It's a low-risk offer. I recommend having a system in place (that you communicate to him) before you begin, as well as communicating when you will check in with him on the progress each day. This can be a great way to slowly ease into taking on more responsibility while building trust.

Ultimately, to get your Executive to relinquish control, you have to lead him to trust your capabilities and your judgment. As you begin to take more and more off his plate (and continue to overdeliver), he will begin to trust you to take on even more—until he eventually realizes that you, in fact, can do it better than he can.

OWN YOUR PART

After you've asked yourself why and identified what may be causing your Executive to be controlling, it's time to turn the mirror on yourself, reflect on your own behavior, and own your part of the situation that you're in. Ask yourself the following questions:

- Am I fulfilling the needs of my Executive?
- Am I achieving the goals and expectations of my position and of the company? Do I even know what the goals and expectations are?
- Do I need to work on my leadership skills?
- Do I need to work on my communication skills?
- What skill might I be lacking that is causing my Executive not to have confidence in me?
- Have I proactively reached out to my Executive to have a conversation with him about me assuming more responsibility and autonomy?

If there are areas where you can improve, start working on those immediately. Revisit this list in thirty days, and do an internal check to see if the micromanaging has improved. If you need to better understand the goals and expectations, ask! If you want more responsibility, ask (or better yet, just do it)! Your Executive has a lot on his plate, and your day-to-day work (or lack thereof) is probably not on his radar. If you want more challenging work and more out of your career, ask for it! Just make sure you deliver.

We will explore the other key components of how to get your boss to give up control (communication, trust, managing and leading up, and joining the inner circle) throughout the rest of this section.

ACHIEVE MORE TOGETHER

- What are you holding on to that you know you could leverage to your Executive Assistant?
- What is stopping you from delegating?
- What is your Executive holding on to? What is stopping them from giving you more projects or responsibility? Why?
- What can you take off your Executive's plate? What is stopping you from taking those projects or tasks from them?
- What are your Executive's patterns? When do they start micromanaging?
- Have you shared with your leader your skills, your strengths, and how best to work with you?
- Review and answer the questions under "Own Your Part."
- Schedule a meeting to discuss other projects your Executive Assistant can handle for you. Include expectations and deadlines in the conversation. During that meeting, your Executive Assistant can also share their experience and strengths, as well as what has worked well for other Executives they've worked with in the past.

COMMUNICATE LIKE A BOSS

Executives, I don't care what form of communication you are using—whether you're Slacking, emailing, texting, or Zooming—just make sure you are communicating with your Executive Assistant regularly. Hallie and I email constantly and also have one face-to-face priority check and direction-setting meeting each week. Our offices are right next to each other, with our Executive Assistant in the middle, so I share ideas and follow up on projects with them in person between meetings. Regular communication will ensure you are always on the same page. Priorities shift constantly, and what may have been important on a Monday may not be by Wednesday. In order for your EA to do her job effectively, she must know about these changes so she can adjust, reschedule meetings, or stop working on one project and shift to the next. Cut down on chaos, and communicate!

Establishing your cadence of communication and your communication channels will enhance your effectiveness. For example, will you meet twice a week, email between meetings, and only use text in emergencies? Or do you prefer text, daily in-person check-ins, and phone calls in case of emergencies only? The means of nication doesn't really matter as long as you establish some cadence of communication between yourself and your EA.

Your Executive Assistant is one of the most important people in your company. She's helping you run the office, your business, and your life. She's supporting your every move and making you look your best along the way. It is critical that you are meeting with your EA at least weekly (I recommend a weekly thirty-minute to one-hour meeting on Monday to go over the week's objectives). Most importantly, never cancel your weekly one-to-one meeting with your Executive Assistant. If she is going to fulfill the needs of her position and ensure that your life and the business operate flawlessly, then she needs to have one-to-one time with you to gather information and understand the priorities of the week or quarter so she can go forth and execute.

Furthermore, your EA's success is intimately tied to helping you with your workload and multiplying your efforts. While a talented EA doesn't need daily direction, she is going to feel disconnected if she is not at least touching base with you regularly on special projects or high-priority items to keep everything moving forward. In addition, most top EAs are dynamic leaders in their own right. If they are not paired with a leader who's at least as strong as them (if not stronger), they will likely leave to work with a leader who they can actually learn and grow from. Suffice it to say that if you want to keep a talented EA on your team, you are going to have to be constantly upping your leadership game. Talent wants to be surrounded by talent. Making time to coach and mentor your Executive Assistant will go a long way toward building a strategic business partnership that will withstand the test of time (and your idiosyncrasies).

KEEPING THE COMMUNICATION FLOWING

For the EA, being a strategic partner means owning and managing all communication. This can be a daunting task. We are fully immersed in the digital age and therefore constantly connected—between email, Facebook Messenger, LinkedIn, text, phone, Zoom, Slack, blogs, Instagram, and more. For the Executive Assistant, it's doubled because EAs are also responsible for managing their Executive's communication channels.

Having a system in place to ensure no communication is missed is the first step. I would recommend filtering as much communication as possible into one place (which often means training people to communicate with you and your Executive via only one or two channels). In our case, email is preferred.

After that, you've got to time block checking the rest of the social media, texts, and messaging apps. Twice a day should suffice. From there, bring it back to email as much as possible. If people reach out on Facebook, Hallie quickly responds (as herself on my behalf) and asks for their email to get them the info they need, as well as giving them her email address in case they want to follow up. Taking control of the communication and gathering information and requests into one place are critical. From there, you can start triaging and responding as needed.

Communicating like a boss (your boss) starts with understanding the expectations around communication. Does your Executive prefer only face-to-face meetings with you and other stakeholders? Does he live and die by text? Does he expect emails to be responded to within three hours or less? Get clear on how he wants to communicate with you and how he wants others to communicate with him, as it will be your job to flawlessly facilitate that communication (including the speed at which it happens).

I also believe proximity can be power. This isn't the case for all Executives, but it is my preferred method of working with my Force Multipliers. For example, while much of my communication with Hallie takes place during our weekly one-to-one meetings, during various company leadership meetings, and via email, nothing can replace the quick pop-in to her office where I can share a brilliant idea I just had (and Hallie can immediately start executing). Or sometimes I want to stop in and download after a particular call or, better yet, grab Hallie and have her listen in on said impromptu call so she can take action immediately. My Executive Assistant is right outside my office. She is able to intercept any drop-ins and can usually help the person out without disturbing my daily schedule. That can't be replaced with a remote assistant (yet).

UNDERSTANDING HOW THE EXECUTIVE COMMUNICATES

Communicating like a boss also means understanding exactly how your Executive communicates, especially if you are going to be drafting emails, memos, social media posts, reports, speeches, and more on his behalf. You must make sure you're reflecting his tone and specific word choice, on top of making sure the message and content are accurate. It's a tall order, but there are several ways to shorten the learning curve rather than just waiting for time to pass and picking it up along the way.

1. **Emails:** Access to the Executive's email is an Executive Assistant's secret weapon. Seriously. It is the fastest way to learn what is happening in the business, how the Executive commu-

nicates, the language he uses, who he responds to, and what he deletes. I know it has helped Hallie learn my leadership and communication styles and how to ask great questions, make better decisions, and even how to lead.

2. **Meetings:** This extends to Zoom video chats, phone calls, and in-person meetings. Attend as many as you can. Listen to how your Executive responds to questions, what questions he is asking, and when he pauses or defers a decision until he has more information. Does he keep it formal and stick strictly to business, or does he prefer a more casual feel with some humor thrown in?

3. **Trainings and Presentations:** If your Executive conducts a lot of training events, speeches, or public appearances, shadow him. Better yet, review past training materials, his blog posts, or his YouTube videos to understand his public persona and the nuances of communication when he is presenting to a larger or more public audience. Again, how does he work a room? Does he facilitate interaction and encourage questions and an open dialogue? How does he follow up?

Be purposeful in your approach to studying your Executive's communication. Mastering his communication style will allow you to adopt it and adapt it when necessary.

One final note on communication. It is not your Executive's responsibility to adjust his communication style to match yours. Say you prefer kid gloves and email and he prefers direct, face-to-face communication. Guess what. You're getting direct, face-to-face communication. Go into your Executive's office, and learn to directly communicate. Your job is to adjust to and accommodate your Executive's work style to multiply his reach, not to change it or him.

Executives and Executive Assistants, here are some tools to enhance your communication.

BEHAVIOR AND PERSONALITY ASSESSMENTS

If you haven't taken a behavior assessment before or haven't taken one in a while, go take one now! There are several free versions online, like the DiSC profile or 16Personalities, as well as paid options, such as Myers-Briggs, CliftonStrengths, the Enneagram test, or the activity vector analysis assessment (AVA).

There is no denying that understanding yourself can greatly enhance your effectiveness. Behavior and personality assessments are a great place to start. They help you understand how you operate under stress and how you address conflict (or avoid it). They help you better understand how you communicate and how you may come across to others. They help clarify how risk tolerant you are, how impatient you can be, how you process information, and much, much more. From that baseline of understanding, you can better operate in the world around you and communicate with others, particularly in business.

But before you read too much into your behavior and personality assessment results, know this: they are not 100 percent accurate or fail-proof. Take the results with a grain of salt, and use them as a tool for self-inquiry, reflection, and conversation. Use the assessments to guide a discussion with your EA or leadership team to get to know each other better and learn how best to work together for maximum results.

Leaders and Force Multipliers should review their assessments together. Figure out where you align and what areas could create conflict in the future. Perhaps your leader is incredibly impatient and likes to charge ahead, while you are more cautious and like to have time to process before taking action. That is really great information to have! You will better understand where your leader is coming from when working on projects, and you can clearly ask for what you need (one hour or one day!) to come back with a plan of action. It may also give you a roadmap for how you need to adjust your communication style or prioritization to better match your leader's natural style. Because I hate to break it to you: it will be up to you, the Force Multiplier, to adjust to your leader's behavioral style, not the other way around!

Now, you don't want your Executive Assistant to have the exact same strengths as you—or else you wouldn't need each other! But there are some key places you will want to align. You will need to determine what those are for yourself and your career. Here's an example: I am a Di personality, which means I'm direct, fast-paced, gregarious, a driver, and an influencer. Hallie is a DC, which means she also works quickly and is direct (and can handle my direct style), but she also has the organizational, detail-oriented, perfectionistic qualities I lack. If she was not a high D personality just like me, she probably wouldn't have lasted working with me for over a decade (she simply would have been bored!).

See why self-awareness is so important? Once you do the hard inner work to understand yourself, you are able to operate from a completely different place—a place filled with confidence and clarity, a combination that makes you unstoppable.

USER'S MANUAL

Another communication tool we use is the User's Manual. In fact, it's one of the very first things we share with any new leadership-team member. The User's Manual is basically a cheat sheet that outlines my idiosyncrasies, values, strengths, and weaknesses. Actually, we talk about all of these things before we even bring someone into our organization. I don't ever want there to be any surprises for people when they join my company. I am a hard-driving, obsessively growth-oriented, high-standards, results-not-stories, push-you-until-you-almost-break-because-I-want-you-to-reach-your-potential kind of guy. For example, I'm not going to sit around with my team and chitchat with them about their weekend, but I will be their biggest ally in their personal and professional growth. Ultimately, I care more about my team's success than I do about being their friend. Not everyone is going to like that. And that's okay. I have had each of my leadership team members complete a User's Manual as well, and we go over them together periodically. Everyone needs a refresher every once in a while, especially when tension is high or we're just not quite on the same page. By knowing where everyone stands, you can all move forward together, faster, without allowing your perception to warp the facts in front of you.

THE FIVE DAILY ACCOUNTABILITY QUESTIONS

The Five Daily Accountability Questions is another communication tool we use with all of our team members. I have all of my direct reports email me their questions at the end of every day. In turn, they have their staff members email these questions to them, and so on throughout the organization. It creates a really great cadence of accountability.

Here are the Five Daily Accountability Questions:

1. What successes did you or your team have today?
2. What struggles did you or your team have today?
3. How did you overcome them?
4. Where is your mindset on a scale of 1–10? (1 being terrible. Be

honest here. I don't care if it's a 1, but if there is something preventing you from being at the top of your game, we need to know and fix it.)

5. What is your next opportunity for growth? What would you like to learn next?

WHY THESE QUESTIONS?

Why these questions? Primarily because they are fast and effective for both you and your staff. In a fast-paced, growing organization, it's hard to have contact with the CEO, director, or supervisor every day. Everyone has a lot on their plate. These questions serve as a daily touchpoint for the leader and employee. People often open up more on email, too, which begins to build trust. More often than not, the answers I receive to these questions have much less to do with the day-to-day operations of the business and more to do with where the employee's mindset is or what is going on in their personal life. Your employees' personal lives do bleed into their work lives, even if they don't talk about it. Be aware and show that you care about what they learned, what they failed at, how they are feeling, and how they are coping with it (at home and at the office).

These questions help you stay aware of the pulse on the people who report to you, especially when you are traveling, you're in all-day trainings, or you simply aren't able to spend time walking around to feel the energy in the office (hello, WFH life!). These daily questions are a system to ensure that you stay in the know, even if you aren't physically there. From there, you are able to direct the energy of your team. Since your EA has access to your email, she should pay attention to these as well. She may be able to find a solution faster than you or simply give extra time and attention to an employee in need.

The last question is designed to get your team members thinking about future opportunities for their growth. If every day they are identifying ways to improve or things they would like to learn, it elevates the entire organization and perpetuates a growth mindset.

More than anything, these questions are a tool for your team. Yes, it is a quick way to gauge your team members' mindsets, pain points, and progress, but it's an even better tool for them to increase their self-awareness. This daily reflection focuses your employees on what they learned and what they could do better tomorrow...and every day. It's a forced journaling model for them to follow. Growth for them is simply inevitable! This is exactly what I'm after as a leader.

IMPLEMENTING THE FIVE QUESTIONS

Here are some key strategies to consider when you start to use the Five Daily Accountability Questions:

- Start these questions on day one with new employees. Set the precedent that their growth is valuable to you and to the organization.
- If you are implementing these questions with existing team members, take the time to explain the why behind it. Give your team a couple of weeks to adjust to the new expectation as well. They will get into a rhythm of answering the questions and being more and more vulnerable and transparent over time.
- Make sure you are replying to each email. Take this seriously. Your employees are taking the time to answer these questions daily, and you're going to hear some very personal (and professional) business struggles. This is exactly what you want! It's impossible for the two not to go hand in hand. Be prepared to

respond with care and candor, and allow your employees the space to be honest and vulnerable. If you don't reply to the emails, the value loop begins to erode, and your team members may stop submitting their Five Daily Accountability Questions. After all, if you're not going to respond, what's the point of them doing them?

- You are not looking for any specific answers to the questions here but rather for patterns of behavior and problems that you need to help solve. For example, if one staff member's mindset is always at an 8 (they'll never be a 10), then when you see her drop to a 5, you know something is up. Conversely, you'll have team members who are always at a 10, so dropping to an 8 or even a 9 could be a red flag. Other questions you might ask yourself as you are reviewing their responses include: Were they able to solve their own challenges or did they blame others? Are they taking responsibility for missed deadlines? Are they learning and progressing each week? All of these questions (and the patterns that emerge) are simply a model to help you be a better leader.
- You're also looking for patterns among your leadership team members. Often, they will be working on the same project or experiencing the same challenge, but they may have vastly different views on the best course of action. As a leader, you must triangulate all of the information and make a decision that best serves the company.

These are powerful and valuable questions, whether you travel three weeks out of the month or are in an office with just one other employee. Add these into your cadence of accountability with your team, and watch your relationships grow and your team members flourish—no watercooler conversation necessary.

HALLIE NARRATES: FIERCE CONVERSATIONS FOR EXECUTIVE ASSISTANTS

One of the books we recommend most often to Executive Assistants and Chiefs of Staff is *Fierce Conversations: Achieving Success at Work & in Life, One Conversation at a Time*, by Susan Scott. Truly, though, it is a book that any leader who wants to achieve results through others should read.

So what is a fierce conversation? It's a conversation when you are present, authentic, and engaging in real dialogue. You are getting to the heart of the matter. You are asking questions, listening, and enriching the relationship, and leaving the conversation with more clarity or a different perspective. The goal of a fierce conversation is to interrogate reality, provoke learning, tackle tough challenges, and enrich relationships. Sounds like something we all should know more about!

Below are the seven key principles of fierce conversations and how they specifically apply to Force Multipliers.

1. Master the Courage to Interrogate Reality

There are three sides to every story: my version, your version, and the truth. As a Force Multiplier, being able to see a situation from numerous angles and make the best decision for your Executive and your organization is a skill. It may not always be what you want to hear (often it means looking at yourself and where you may have come up short), but ultimately it means progress. In addition to hearing things that may be hard to hear, you need to be able to say things that are hard to say. Being a truth-teller to your Executive and leadership team is a key skill to leading up and being an influential leader. What you have always believed to be true just may not be the case. By bringing these issues into the light, you can have real conversations and make real progress.

It takes courage. It takes the ability to let go of the outcome and know that what you are doing is coming from a place of curiosity and a desire to create a better relationship or company. And it's worth it.

2. Come Out from behind Yourself Into the Conversation, and Make It Real

Authenticity is the answer in today's business world. Well, at least it is in ours, and I hope it is at your company too. You can get a lot more done, faster, and with much more career satisfaction when you are bringing your whole self to work, sharing your ideas, bringing issues to light, and sharing your perspective. Who wants to go to work every day suppressing parts of themselves? It is a disservice to your Executive, your company, and ultimately to yourself.

It's impossible to accomplish your goals if you don't make every conversation as honest and transparent as possible. Have you ever gone into a meeting with noble intentions of saying what's on your mind and finally making progress on an issue that has been bugging you for months, yet when the meeting ended, you left without getting your point across? Don't let fear hold you back. Laying the issues out on the table with direct and honest communication will get results.

3. Be Here, Prepared to Be Nowhere Else

As Executive Assistants, two of our most powerful skills are listening and observing. We are often the eyes and ears of the organization and need to be able to succinctly communicate the pulse of the organization back to our Executive. But that is impossible to do if we are rushing from one meeting to the next with our heads down scrolling through emails on our iPhones. Susan Scott said it best: "Our work, our relationships, and our lives succeed or fail one conversation at a time. While no single conversation is guaranteed to transform a company, a relationship, or a life, any single conversation can." Being present means putting away your phone, moving away from your computer, and even just mentally and emotionally preparing yourself for a conversation. Clear your physical space and clear your mind so that you are 100 percent with that person in that moment.

4. Tackle Your Toughest Challenge Today

You know what it is. It's that project or conversation that you have been avoiding, hoping that it would resolve on its own. It didn't. More often than not, your toughest challenge is going to be a tough conversation with your Executive or leadership team. Perhaps it's time to talk with your Executive about being a control freak. Maybe it's time to ask for a raise or you need to let an employee go. Regardless of the issue, it never helps to wait. Most problems can be solved faster, with longer-term results, when done in the moment or as soon as possible. By waiting to have the conversation, you are setting a precedent that the behavior or the situation is okay with you. When you finally confront the issue six months later, it can cause confusion and resentment. Don't wait. Confront obstacles in your path and accomplish more!

5. Obey Your Instincts

How many times have you gone against your intuition, only to regret it later? Pay attention to your gut, and listen to your inner voice. Your gut reactions are often subconscious responses to your previous experiences. Gather information and know the facts, but obey your instincts.

There are ways to approach a conversation that allow you to obey your instincts and interrogate reality with professionalism, respect, and curiosity. For example, if I have noticed an issue a few times with my Executive, I might grab them for a one-to-one (when they are not busy or distracted, but also in a timely manner), and say, "I'm prepared to be wrong here, but here is what I am noticing and how it could be perceived. What are your thoughts?" If I were giving feedback to an employee or colleague, I might say, "I noticed XYZ, and I think it could be perceived as [fill in the blank] or is making other people feel [fill in the blank]. What are you seeing from your perspective?"

If you know something needs to be addressed or said, say it. But remember, there are always multiple sides to a story. Enter the conversation with curiosity and a desire to understand. You will get a lot further with the individual, and you will likely learn something along the way.

6. Take Responsibility for Your Emotional Wake

When entering into a fierce conversation, you have to check your energy and emotions at the door. This doesn't mean that you are a robot or emotionless, but bringing your own agenda or emotional charge to the conversation is not helpful for anyone. Maintaining a neutral state, staying curious, listening, digging deeper, and helping yourself and the individual come to some sort of resolution is important.

As a Force Multiplier, you have significant influence over your Executive, your leadership team, and the company at large. You must be hypervigilant about what you say and, more importantly, how you act. For you, there is no trivial comment, just as there isn't for your Executive. Something you may have said in passing may actually carry a lot of weight to the people in your organization. Choose your words and tone wisely because while people might not remember exactly what you said, they will remember how you made them feel.

7. Let Silence Do the Heavy Lifting

Sometimes the most meaningful conversations have the fewest words.

If you ask a question, do not rush to fill the silence, but rather, allow the space for someone to actually answer your question. If you ask your Executive a pointed question, stop and wait for a response. It is incredibly hard not to dive in and start talking, clarifying, or asking another question. Or sometimes we just fill the silence with meaningless chatter because the silence is uncomfortable. Slow down the conversation to allow for reflection and thoughtful responses. Allow the silence and the space, and listen for what isn't being said. Are they processing? How is their body language? How long are the pauses? If you can just wait out the silence, what comes out on the other side can be massive ahas, insights, thought-provoking questions, or incredible ideas or answers that could change the trajectory of the relationship, the company, or both.

When was the last time you had a fierce conversation? What conversation have you been avoiding? Who do you really need to have a conversation with right now? Schedule it! Tackle it today, and get it on the calendar. Success in work and life happens one conversation at a time. Get talking. Get fierce. Get results.

Strong communication between a leader and a Force Multiplier makes all the difference when building a successful strategic partnership. It's the foundation from which the rest of the organization learns, takes their cues, and gets much of their information. Being in sync and intentional about creating a communication framework will have you and your Executive Assistant communicating like a boss in no time.

ACHIEVE MORE TOGETHER

- Each of you should complete a behavior assessment and use it as a starting point for self-inquiry, as well as a conversation about how best to work together.
- Complete User's Manuals, and discuss them with each other.
- Schedule a weekly one-to-one meeting with your Force Multiplier. Don't cancel or schedule over it!
- Discuss and agree upon your preferred communication channels.
- Implement the Five Daily Accountability Questions.

SET CLEAR GOALS, EXPECTATIONS, AND WINS

Once you have your communication channels and cadence of communication down with your Executive Assistant, it's time to turn your attention to communicating clear goals, expectations, and wins. When you're working with your sales team or your operations staff, the goals are pretty clear: hit your numbers. X number in sales volume or X number of leads generated or X ROI. Simple, right? Well, what about the goals and expectations for your assistant? How does she know she's meeting your expectations? How does she know she is winning with you? How do you each measure success in the role?

Executive Assistants' and Force Multipliers' goals can often be overlooked or maybe not even taken into consideration as we go about goal setting for ourselves or the organization. But we're here to change that.

It is just as important for Executive Assistants, Chiefs of Staff, and other Force Multipliers to establish their personal and professional goals each year. Yes, they may be closely tied to their Executive's or company's goals; in fact, they generally should be. However, you must get clear on—and establish a way to measure—their unique goals and contributions. Why? Because it helps you help your EA to create a path for their career growth, and it gives you both clear information when discussing a promotion or compensation increase.

So while I don't have an exact goal or "win" for you to implement with your assistant, make sure *you* have one. Discuss it, and get your assistant's buy-in. Maybe it's the number of client reviews you receive each month. Maybe it's ensuring that the employee morale rating is at 90 percent at all times. Perhaps it is simply that emails are caught up on and there are no outstanding action items at the end of each week.

What does a win look like for me and my EA? It means that once I have handed off a task, idea, or project, the expectation is that it does not come back across my desk until it is complete. The win is for me to be able to clear my head of those tasks and trust that my EA will take ownership and get it done.

In Hallie's role as Chief of Staff, she measures success a little bit differently. First, she measures success based on whether my goals and the company's goals are being met. In addition, she measures success by identifying gaps in the organization and bringing new ideas, perspectives, and solutions to me or other team members. And finally, she measures success by how much she is learning, growing, and contributing. We have discussed how she measures success, and I agree—which is a win for both of us.

The point here is to have some sort of standard and target that your

Force Multiplier can work on achieving and exceeding. Take it a step further and also outline clear "rewards" (bonuses, tuition reimbursement, equity, etc.). No matter how awesome you are, your assistant will likely need more inspiration and motivation than simply serving at the pleasure of the CEO.

ACHIEVE MORE TOGETHER

- What are your goals?
- What are your expectations for your Force Multiplier?
- What are your Force Multiplier's goals?
- How do you measure success for your Force Multiplier?
- How does your Force Multiplier measure success?
- Are you and your Force Multiplier on the same page with what success looks like?
- How does your Force Multiplier win with you? How do you win with your Force Multiplier?
- How does your Force Multiplier lose with you? How do you lose with your Force Multiplier?
- Do you have an incentive or bonus structure in place for your Force Multiplier? What is it?

BOUNDARIES AND WORK-LIFE PRESENCE

An important part of setting clear expectations with your Executive Assistant comes down to when, where, and how she works. Enter the boundaries conversation.

There is an interesting dichotomy in the professional world. On one hand we've got the "workaholics," and on the other we've got those individuals in constant search of work-life balance. The workaholics scoff at the idea of "balance," and those who seek balance don't understand the relentless obsession of the workaholics. Who's right? Who's wrong? Well, it's not as simple as that. In both cases, I actually think that what people are searching for is meaningful work and being present in the moment.

Some individuals are driven and fueled by their chosen profession—it could be their calling, a desire to prove themselves to their family, or simply a need for a certain title or income. It's about the work and what the work means for them—whatever the reason. Work often comes first, and those individuals (who some may call workaholics) are unapologetic about it. They don't feel the need for a break from work because they typically enjoy what they do and don't consider it work. Whether they are engaged in a side hustle, on year seven of their high-growth startup, training to become a professional athlete, or on the fast track to making partner, those people find meaning and fulfillment in their work. It may mean extremely long hours, personal sacrifices, and working nights and weekends, but again, for their own reasons, it works for them.

Those in the work-life balance camp are looking for more separation, more boundaries between work and life. They are unapologetic about protecting their time out of the office. Up until around the 1980s, work-life balance wasn't even part of our lexicon. It was just how the professional world worked. Most of the working population went to work and came home, and that was that. Very few took work home with them. Unless they were getting phone calls on their landlines or receiving faxes at home, they were largely disconnected once they left the office. For the past thirty-plus years, as smartphones have gotten smarter and the competitive edge more competitive, the lines between "work" and "home" have blurred (not to mention the whole workplace shift during the COVID-19 pandemic!). Some individuals tend to embrace this world. Work anytime from anywhere—great! Meanwhile the work-life balance individuals are rebelling against this new norm. Again, who's right and who's wrong?

I tend to fall somewhere in the middle. I believe there is a time and place for long hours and an all-consuming focus on work. In fact, my company is at a place in its growth where we need that level of commitment from our team. There's no need to urge those individuals to work harder, answer emails "after hours," or help out with a project on the weekend. They are already there, sleeves rolled up, ready to get dirty and get the job done. The challenge I tend to have with my team is getting them to leave the office at a reasonable hour or take a vacation. In my opinion, that's not a bad problem to have.

WHAT IS WORK-LIFE PRESENCE?

When it comes to work-life balance, I believe in work-life presence. Here's what work-life presence means to me: it's the daily integration of learning, working, and playing, and being fully present throughout each interaction. Now, before you get hung up on the playing part, remember, it doesn't mean your play needs to be seven hours a day. It can be thirty minutes or an hour or two, depending on the day. The key is that each day you are putting intentional focus on learning and growing, working hard on the most important task or project that will have the biggest impact on your business or job, and playing and enjoying life. As a leader, it's my job to make sure that my team is constantly touching all three of these areas each day, integrating their work, lives, families, and growth as much as possible day after day until it is a continuous loop of consistent growth.

After all, there are 168 hours in the week, and those people who are after work-life balance aren't looking to work 84 hours a week! And neither am I. I believe that if we are aligned with our natural behavior and doing work that fulfills us (no matter how many hours a week we do it), we're not going to feel burned out, nor are we going to be searching for more balance. If we're in alignment, it's just going to feel right.

In concept, all of this sounds great. But this idea of work-life presence or work-life balance probably affects the Executive and the Executive Assistant more than anyone else in the organization. Because the work of the EA is so closely tied to that of the Executive, what are the parameters of a workday? If a Founder is working at all hours of the day and night, does the Executive Assistant have to too? How does this integration, presence, and balance work for EAs and their Executives?

SETTING BOUNDARIES

Well, now would be as good a time as any to discuss boundaries. As one who is fueled by freedom, I cringe just a little bit at the concept of boundaries. All I hear is scarcity, restrictions, and limits. But the logical side of me knows that boundaries are really less about restriction and more about creating a mutually agreed-upon structure within which to operate with maximum productivity. Just as discipline equals freedom, structure and boundaries also equal freedom. I can get behind that.

One of the first things an Executive must do when hiring an Executive Assistant is set clear boundaries and expectations about what the job entails. What hours do you expect your assistant to be available? How available is available (does she need to be at the office or just have her phone or laptop nearby)? It doesn't necessarily matter what the answer is; you just need to make sure that you and your assistant are on the same page, that there is equitable compensation for the work being asked of the Executive Assistant, and that it works for both of you. It only becomes an issue when you or your assistant starts operating outside of the agreed-upon boundaries and expectations.

I'm an Executive who wants to partner with someone who understands and enjoys a flexible schedule and work-life presence. If you have a more structured day and like to disconnect at 6:00 p.m., then you might get annoyed with someone like Hallie who likes to check in or email articles or new ideas at 9:00 p.m. Again, there is no right or wrong answer, but you have to be in alignment with how you like to work and what the standards and expectations are for your business.

This extends to other standards and expectations, such as travel, night and weekend availability, how involved you expect your EA to be in your personal life, and flexibility with working at the office, from her home, or even from your home. Get clear on how you see the partnership working, and then make sure your EA is on board. If not, it just might not be the right fit.

That's my opinion. Let's get Hallie's perspective too.

HALLIE NARRATES: THE BOUNDARIES CONVERSATION

I used to think boundaries and work-life balance were bullshit. I still think that is true, at least as far as set hours and a structured day are concerned. However, I have a more moderate approach to boundaries these days. Bottom line, I believe that as long as both parties are clear about the expectations and have agreed to a compensation package that encompasses those expectations, then the EA and Exec should be good to go forth and work.

In April 2017, I conducted a survey and asked Executive Assistants around the world, "What is the biggest challenge you are experiencing at home or at the office due to your role as an Executive Assistant?" The overwhelming response was work-life balance and boundaries, followed closely by not having enough hours in the day to handle all of the shifting priorities. A schedule with long, often undefined hours, coupled with multiple competing priorities, is tough. I've been there, and I get it. But here is my (likely) very unpopular opinion: that's the job. That is what an EA does. It's not for everyone.

Now, don't get me wrong, I don't think people should work all the time (and if you are, you'd better be fairly compensated for it!). You need other hobbies. You need to spend time with friends and family, to take care of your mind, body, and spirit. It's not easy for anyone to manage all of life's obligations, and it's particularly difficult for EAs, but it is not impossible.

Ultimately, I think that EAs should make sure they are very clear about what they are getting into (with the caveat that no two EA roles are the same). Some positions may require being available at all times, while some may ask that you simply stay connected via email. Some require extensive travel, and others are simply nine to five, with no requirements outside of those hours. However, I would be skeptical about any position that is simply nine to five (particularly at an executive level). EAs make the life of an Executive flawless, and what Executive do you know who only works between the hours of nine and five? Be aware of what the position entails before signing on.

Now, many of the survey participants also mentioned that they have flexible schedules. Again, they might be in the office from nine to five, but they can run out to their kids' soccer game, a dentist appointment, or lunch with a friend at their discretion. It works both ways. An EA may be up at 2:00 a.m. waiting for her Executive to land in Europe, but she may also leave early on a Friday for a massage.

So why are so many EAs searching for that work-life balance if, in fact, most of the respondents said they love their careers in spite of the hours?

I think it has a lot less to do with balance and much more to do with not feeling in control of their schedules and their time. Very few positions are as demanding and dependent on someone else's direction—someone else's priorities, projects, needs, and deadlines. I believe that with the help of some clear expectations and some extreme time management, inner balance can be restored, even if it still looks out of balance from the outside.

As the Chief of Staff to a serial Entrepreneur, I have done everything from setting up new entities to refining systems that allowed us to launch teams in new states; planning, organizing, and selling tickets for a nonprofit event; reviewing budgets and strategic plans; training other Executive Assistants; recruiting and hiring staff; helping write course content; scheduling meetings and travel; holding other staff members accountable; preparing presentations; and conducting meetings on behalf of my Executive. And, of course, much more.

Regardless of the exact responsibilities Executive Assistants have, I haven't met individuals who work harder to accomplish a mission. While I am no longer Adam's Executive Assistant, when I was, I didn't go to bed unless I knew he had arrived. For example, I emailed with him at 2:00 a.m. before he went off the grid to hike Kilimanjaro. I came into the office on the weekends to work on projects, prepare for events, or move offices. I got out of bed more than once to rearrange travel and get him booked on a new flight after delays or cancellations. It needed to be handled. I handled it.

People who don't quite understand our unique roles may think the Executive is expecting too much or that these requests are unacceptable or intrusive. But what they don't know is that very rarely does the Executive actually have to request that these things happen—the Executive Assistant just does them of her own volition. I knew what I was signing up for; in fact, I thrive on this. I work for an incredibly interesting and dynamic Entrepreneur, and I am helping him build multiple organizations; occasionally work doesn't happen between 9:00 a.m. and 5:00 p.m., Monday through Friday. The trade-off? I get to work for an incredibly interesting and dynamic Entrepreneur and help him build multiple organizations. The work is challenging and rewarding, and it doesn't hurt that I have complete flexibility with my schedule and unlimited vacation and time off.

Depending on what side of the aisle you're on, you either think the Executive Assistant position is incredibly demeaning or incredibly sexy. The reality is somewhere in the middle. It has its really glamorous moments of meeting extraordinary people, traveling, and attending high-stakes meetings, and it has moments where you're picking up trash after an event. You've got to take it all in stride and take the good with the bad. After all, it's about ensuring the flawless implementation of your Executive's personal and professional vision, and there are a lot of things (big and small) that go into making that happen. If you think you are above some of the more menial tasks, you will never survive.

Remember, there is no right or wrong answer to the boundaries question; just make sure you and your Executive are on the same page. You have a right to say no or adjust if it no longer works for you. Just understand that may mean you and your Executive are no longer a match. Regardless, once you have agreed and committed, put on your big-girl pants and execute.

Next, Adam's going to share how to best handle the personal side of an Executive's life.

ON A PERSONAL NOTE

Before you and an Executive Assistant get into business together, it's also important to make sure you understand where each of you stands on the personal side of things. By that I mean will your EA be handling your personal appointments, family travel, and other personal requests? Get clear on what you expect of your EA. Now, most experienced EAs understand that there will be some overlap between the business and personal; however, clarify. Make sure you spell it out, and make sure she agrees.

I'll also note that you want to make sure your significant other is on board with the arrangement too. Your significant other and EA should be allies, not adversaries. Part of your EA's job will be making sure your partner stays informed of your travel schedule, when you'll be out of the country, or simply when you have an early-morning meeting. Conversely, you'll want your partner to communicate with your EA about family parties, soccer games, and anniversary dinners to make sure they are on the calendar and protected. They may also work with each other on holiday card lists, dinner party planning, birthday gifts, family vacations, and more.

Your Executive Assistant should understand your family dynamic and protect your interests not just as an Executive, but as a husband, father, and son. For example, when traveling for business, I often like to bring my family with me and make sure I keep up with my fitness routine. This means my EA needs to know what my training schedule is and whether I'll want a hotel with a pool or a nearby cryotherapy spa, as well as understanding all of the travel preferences of my immediate family.

I recommend that your Executive Assistant and your partner

meet monthly to discuss any upcoming travel or any out-of-the-ordinary meetings that would disrupt the family's daily routine. This monthly check-in is a great time for your EA to note any parent-teacher conferences, birthday parties, or special family events as well.

As I mentioned earlier, there are no right or wrong answers to what you want or need to fulfill your role as a business leader. You simply need to make sure you clearly communicate your expectations and that you and your EA are aligned. You want your EA to not only understand what you need, but also see it as an integral part of her job, not as a burden. Set clear expectations to avoid long-term resentment. You'll both be grateful for it.

ACHIEVE MORE TOGETHER

- What does work-life balance or work-life presence mean to you and your Executive Assistant? Get clear and discuss.
- Is your Force Multiplier clear on your expectations around their schedule and responsibilities? Have they agreed to these expectations?
- Have you each defined your boundaries? If not, schedule a time to discuss, and ensure there is mutual understanding and agreement.
- Will your Executive Assistant be involved in your personal affairs? If so, to what extent? What are the expectations around personal tasks and projects?

BUILD TRUST AND CULTIVATE LOYALTY

Once you have developed some basic structure around your working relationship with your Executive Assistant, established clear communication, and aligned your expectations, it's time to take the partnership to the next level. Trust and loyalty are the cornerstones of a successful EA-Executive strategic partnership; do not just assume they will happen.

Leadership requires you to be intentional about cultivating trust with your team members. Do what you say you will. Be accountable to your words and your actions. Do the right thing, and admit your mistakes. Never throw your assistant under the bus for a mistake you made (though often she will be willing to accept blame and will not mind taking one for the team). Be honest (sometimes brutally so) and vulnerable, and create an environment where your assistant can do the same. Do not allow others to bully or abuse your assistant. Support your EA the way she supports you.

Trust is a fairly subjective behavior, as is loyalty. However, there are some signs to look for when building trust and cultivating loyalty with your Executive Assistant. For example, does she do what she says she is going to do? Does she show up? I don't mean just that she's on time to the office. I mean does she answer your text at 11:00 p.m. when you're traveling? Does your EA check in early before she heads off on vacation? Does your EA keep confidential information confidential? Are you able to rely on her? This doesn't mean that she never makes mistakes, but when she does, does she own them immediately? Does she put her ego aside for you and for the company? Does she clarify misconceptions when appropriate and fiercely protect you, your brand, and your reputation?

Again, this comes with time. But if trust and loyalty are compromised, it could be a long road to building that back up. This goes both ways. You and your EA must both start building trust and loyalty from day one. You must have each other's backs in order for a true partnership to exist.

WITH TRUST COMES LOYALTY

In order for a true strategic partnership to exist, there must be trust between the Executive and the Executive Assistant. It should go without saying, but maintaining strict confidentiality and loyalty are a must. Hallie likes to think of herself as "the protector of Adam and the empire" (cue the Wonder Woman theme song). Hallie says, "I protect Adam's time, his reputation, his family, his brand, his team, his interests, and ultimately the organization. I would not be doing my job if I didn't put Adam first." Now that is the kind of Force Multiplier you should partner with.

Executive Assistants are in a unique position where they have the privilege of learning from and interacting daily with the top Executives in the organization. A large part of an Executive Assistant's role is to act as a gatekeeper. Yet gatekeepers are not meant to keep people out; rather, they should let the right people in at the right time. They should control the flow of information, not stop it. EAs can either hoard information and use that position of power as a crutch, or they can share what they learn with their coworkers and be seen as a leader, resource, and influencer at all levels of the organization. Information should flow up, down, and sideways throughout the company—and this often hinges on the successful communication skills of the EA. That does not mean she should be an open book. The EA's first priority is to maintain the confidentiality and the confidence of the Executive. But understanding what information can and should be shared with which team members is an important part of the EA role.

There is such a fine line between maintaining confidentiality and being closed off. Part of an EA's role is being open and accessible, communicating just enough of the company's mission or the Executive's message to further the goals of the company, while being available to listen and report back to the Executive. Now, this puts Executive Assistants in a very interesting position. Forget about chitchatting around the office and engaging in idle gossip (either in person or online). The EA not only has her own reputation to maintain, but she also must maintain the reputation of her Executive. Her actions will be a direct reflection of the Executive and his brand. If her Executive is in the public eye, she will be under even more scrutiny.

People will try to get to the EA in order to get to the Executive. This doesn't always have to be negative, though. Internal and external stakeholders know that the EA has the Executive's ear, and if they can't get to him, sometimes she's the next best option. That is an honor and a privilege and should not be taken lightly. The EA also may be the go-to in the company for people to express their higher-level concerns. That's okay. She should make listening a priority and be transparent. For example, our team members know that Hallie is a safe space and will maintain strict confidentiality at all times, but she is also very clear that she will share any and all information with me (and only me) as she sees fit. So if they don't want me to know that they are interviewing for other positions outside the company, they probably shouldn't tell Hallie. Hallie's loyalty is to me first. That is how we've built trust.

It's also important that the EA not take advantage of her position in order to receive special treatment, and she should never, ever, speak on behalf of the Executive without his express permission. Being an EA can be an isolating position at times, so it's key for her to surround herself with people outside of the office who understand her job and can support her. Looking for those people inside the organization can be a recipe for disaster. It only takes one too many glasses of wine before the EA is spilling secrets of the C-suite to the Finance Director and destroying any trust she had with her Executive. Reserve those conversations for your close friends and family only. Better yet, have those conversations (i.e., voice those complaints) with your Executive. Right, Hallie?

HALLIE NARRATES: TRUST AND LOYALTY

Exactly. While I can be strategically guarded when dealing with our team or the public, Adam knows me well enough that I can't hide a challenge or problem from him for long. And I wouldn't want to. He's the best person to help me solve it! Adam is not only my boss; he's also my mentor. In our weekly meetings and daily accountability questions, we discuss everything from workouts to career development, our next hires, gun laws, leadership, our family dynamics, witness consciousness, and industry trends. When you build this level of trust, loyalty will inevitably follow. Again, this takes time and commitment, but the payoff is worth it and ultimately results in a stronger partnership.

ACHIEVE MORE TOGETHER

- What does trust mean to you and your Force Multiplier?
- What does loyalty look like for you and your Force Multiplier?
- What elements must exist for you to know you trust your Executive Assistant and that they can trust you?
- Schedule a time to meet and discuss your thoughts and perspectives around trust and loyalty.
- Which element of trust (accountability, reliability, integrity, confidentiality, vulnerability, etc.) do you need to work on first?

THE INNER CIRCLE

The final piece of the strategic partnership puzzle is for your Executive Assistant to earn the right to join the inner circle and for you to invite them into your world.

The Executive Assistant role, much like the role of a leader, can be an isolating and siloed position. I find it interesting that on most organizational charts, the Executive Assistant and/or Chief of Staff are always hanging out on the side by themselves. They don't necessarily have any direct reports, nor are they a part of any one business function (that is, except for the function of handling the Executive's business).

Your assistant works *with* you, not *for* you. Hallie and my Executive Assistant read all of my emails, attend the majority of my classes and trainings, listen in on calls, and sit in on meetings. They are both more effective when they know what I know, how I think, how I solve problems, and what I have decided and promised (so they can follow up and deliver). Do not keep your assistant on the periphery, assigning tasks that have no context or meaning. She will be far more invested in your success when she is a part of the entire process and eventually part of the big decisions or even making decisions on your behalf. When you bring your assistant into your inner circle, everyone wins.

Throughout the rest of this chapter, Hallie will provide Executive Assistants with recommendations on how they can join the inner circle.

HALLIE NARRATES: BE INVALUABLE AND COMMAND ENTRANCE TO THE INNER CIRCLE

Don't deny it. I know you want to be a part of the inner circle. It's an exclusive club composed of respect, trust, and loyalty, and it gives you unlimited access to confidential information and turns you into someone your Executive looks to for advice, knowledge, and expertise on various topics. It's a club with a strict vetting process, and it's up to you to become the Executive Assistant you need to become in order to command a spot in the inner circle. You must earn the right.

Know What Your Executive Knows

The most basic yet one of the most impactful ways to gain entrance into the inner circle is to know what your Executive knows. Simple, right? But not always easy. This goes far beyond knowing how your boss takes his coffee (Note: Adam takes his strong and black but prefers green tea in the afternoon). This habit requires some serious dedication (usually reading or listening to books and podcasts in your "off hours"). But I think it is the most critical habit to develop as an Executive Assistant, and it's something you can implement right away, no matter how new you are to the EA role.

This habit has helped me become an invaluable resource to Adam. If he mentions a book he's reading, I read it. If he is following a blog or podcast, so do I. I watch the movies, read the books, review the annual reports of charities he supports, and listen to the podcasts he does. Why? Because the more I am able to align myself with his interests and, more importantly, his knowledge, the more I am able to not just listen but also converse with him and participate in conversations that he's having with other leadership members or key business partners. He never asked me to do this, but my natural curiosity and thirst for knowledge led me to create this habit from the beginning, and it has truly been invaluable. When he is in a meeting and says, "Who was that quote by?" or "What year did that company go public?" I know. He doesn't have to repeat himself or fill me in on a critical article he read or a book that he would like to discuss at a company meeting—I'm already familiar with it.

Does your Executive read *The Wall Street Journal* or *Inc.* magazine? Get a subscription. Is he watching *Suits* or *Yellowstone*? Watch it. Is he listening to an Adyashanti audio series or *The Tim Ferriss Show*? Listen too. If nothing else, instead of being on the periphery, this will bring you closer to the inner circle. Your Executive will want to be able to discuss the latest episode of *Yellowstone* with you just as much as the most recent article on Jeff Bezos. Be ready and able to participate in and add value to the conversation. This is such a simple habit to implement, yet it's one that will set you apart and help you grow that much faster.

Study Your Executive

As a Force Multiplier, the more I can align my knowledge and thinking with Adam's, the more valuable I become to him and the company. Executive Assistants are responsible for furthering the reach of their Executives. Often that means completing tasks and projects that, while important, are not the best use of their Executive's time. More often, it means making decisions and speaking on behalf of their boss. The most effective way to do that is by having the same information as the Executive and thoroughly understanding the way he thinks. Yes, some of this will come with time. But start right away! Gain as much knowledge as possible. Study his emails and responses to questions. Listen in on phone calls (get permission first!). Attend as many meetings as possible. Be able to speak your Executive's language. Beyond that, you'll also be learning how he thinks, makes decisions, and leads. This will allow you not only to be a part of the conversation but, eventually, to be able to speak and lead on his behalf with accuracy and authority.

Learn the Business

It's one thing to do your job and another thing altogether to do your job really, really well within the context of your company and industry. Executive Assistant positions are relatively similar in their daily functions but can be drastically different based on the Executive or the industry you are operating in. So as much as you can learn about the business, do that! Be ready to lead and ready to follow. Hone your business acumen. Ask questions and be engaged.

One way to go about learning the business is by studying each major division and understanding how they operate. How does the company make money? What is the life cycle of a customer? What are your target markets? Does the company plan to expand their operations any time soon? If so, how and where? What are the current operational challenges? How does the Human Resources department manage career development and create an engaging culture?

If possible, I would recommend shadowing each department and even going through the onboarding process for a new sales executive, operations manager, customer service team member, finance director, etc. You could get a great glimpse into how each division operates by getting the initial run-through. You'll also learn who your go-to colleagues will be in the future and what challenges each division is facing.

Of course, if you can attend the various department meetings and all-leadership meetings, do that too. Learn the industry, and learn the business and, more importantly, how your role plays into the overall success of the division or company. Couple that with a clear understanding of your Executive's thought process and communication style, and you will be unstoppable.

Plan and Prepare

Another way to command entrance into the inner circle is to plan, prepare, and be resourceful. Advanced planning is a term I picked up from my husband. It's often used by law enforcement officers or the military to refer to pre-mission preparations, such as the President visiting a foreign country or preparing a tactical team to infiltrate a hostile environment. While the stakes aren't usually as high for you and your Executive, no matter how big or small the project, I want you to think of yourself as a one-person advanced-planning team. So much planning and preparation goes into play to ensure your Executive has a flawless presentation or even just has a flawless day at the office. From meeting prep to travel arrangements, board meetings, and event planning, part of leading up means planning extensively, preparing for any eventuality, and then being resourceful when it all goes wrong.

Prior to any meeting, phone call, interview, event, speech, etc., you should research and prepare (actually, over-prepare) information and notes to best equip your Executive. Most of this information will include detailed bios, company information, or recent news pieces or awards. You want your Executive going into the meeting or interview fully understanding who he is meeting and how that person fits into the overall objectives of the organization. Often, this information is more for you to study than for the Executive. He will likely want a quick brief prior to a meeting or event, but if you don't do your research, you won't have the answers. To that point, make sure you are clear on what the meeting or call is about and what point your Executive will be presenting. You may need to pull additional reports from the sales team or data from the finance department.

In addition to hard data and information, much of your Executive's day is spent dealing with people problems or last-minute requests. In these instances, you'll want to understand the issue at hand as much as possible. This could mean talking to the members involved first and then relaying as much information as possible to your Executive—including the person's attitude, tone, and agenda—prior to the meeting. Bonus points for coming with a proposed solution to how your Executive could deal with an upset employee or a disgruntled client.

Be Resourceful

Finally, be resourceful. Know who to go to with questions when you get stuck. Understand how you can get to the desired outcome in a different way. No matter how much planning takes place, something is going to go wrong. Hopefully, you have a Plan B, Plan C, and Plan D in place and have worked through a few other contingency plans in your mind. But when you're in the moment, sometimes no matter how good the plan, you've got to scrap it and just act. Fight or flight? You've got to fight through to make it happen. Being resourceful is simply another way to say, "Get it done!"

Ultimately, one of the best ways to join the inner circle is to master the art of leading (i.e., managing) up. The topic of leadership warrants its own section. Read on as Adam explains how to increase your leadership skills and the art of leading up.

ACHIEVE MORE TOGETHER

- Do you have a strategic partnership with your leader/Force Multiplier? Why or why not?
- What must you each learn or do in order to build that strategic partnership and meet each other in the inner circle?
- Force Multipliers, what else can you do to better align your thinking with your Executive's? What else do you need to learn about the business?

PART THREE

LEADERSHIP IS INFLUENCE

LEADING WITHOUT A TITLE

For Executive Assistants, understanding how to discuss problems with your Executive, working on being a well-rounded asset, and understanding your Executive's goals are all critical to being a successful strategic partner and gaining entrance to the inner circle. By making yourself invaluable, you will command a seat at the table. And the fastest way to become an invaluable asset is to learn how to lead your Executive.

Quick note: While the more common terminology is *managing up*, we like to talk about *leading up*. You manage systems, but you lead people. So if you really want to help your Executive, you want to lead him, not manage him. Believe me, no one wants to be managed, least of all your Executive.

LEADING AND ASSISTING

Executive Assistants are in an interesting situation where they don't have the traditional title of a leader, yet they're required to act in a leadership capacity much of the time. The challenges of this situation are compounded by the fact that many people still misunderstand the EA position and don't want to deal with the "assistant." While Hallie and I both think that perception is changing, the change really starts with the EAs. They must learn to navigate these murky waters and develop influence. Influential, not positional, leadership is what truly separates great leaders from average leaders.

In his book *High Performance Habits,* Brendon Burchard notes the three things one must do to develop influence:

1. Teach people how to think about themselves, about others, and about the world.
2. Role-model the values you wish to see others embody.
3. Challenge others to develop their character, connections, and contributions.

To develop influence, you must build the habits of a capable and confident leader and then role-model that behavior. If you want others to look to you as a leader, then you must show up as one every day. To develop influence, you have to teach other people how to think. Much of this comes through coaching, training, and, again, role-modeling the behavior. Provide a safe yet challenging place for people to come to help them work through their thinking, and then hold them accountable for taking action. Push your team members. Issue them challenges, and see who rises to the occasion. Regardless of your title, when you are challenging others to think differently and to become the best versions of themselves by trying new things and getting out of their comfort zone, you can't help but be seen as a leader.

So what does this look like in real life? Well, an EA likely knows the goals of various team members. She may even know the goals and dreams of external stakeholders. How can she cultivate those dreams? Maybe she checks in with a VP each week to see how her Spartan Sprint training is going. Maybe she engages in a discussion with the director of HR to encourage him to consider alternative recruiting options. Maybe she challenges an EA in another company to participate in Toastmasters with her. Maybe she plays devil's advocate with the sales manager so he better understands the client's perspective.

Developing influence is a practice and an art. EAs must commit to the process of developing their leadership and practice it at every opportunity. Leading without a title isn't without its challenges, but the rewards are immense. Make it easier by working on your executive presence.

ACHIEVE MORE TOGETHER

- What does influential leadership look like in your organization?
- Are you role-modeling the behaviors you wish to see in your employees, leaders, and coworkers?
- The next time you disagree with your leader, ask questions and respectfully challenge their thinking. Offer alternative viewpoints and solutions.
- Force Multipliers, flex your leadership skills by offering to lead a committee or oversee the implementation of a new initiative.
- Take one concept from this book and share it with another Force Multiplier or leader.

EXECUTIVE PRESENCE FOR EXECUTIVE ASSISTANTS

Ah, executive presence. The often-elusive leadership coaching catchphrase. What is it, and why do you need it? Executive presence is quite a broad term and yet one of the key skills leaders must master at all levels of an organization. Executive presence is not just for CEOs or "Executives." It is not something you are born with but rather a leadership skill that can be developed over time. Yes, that means Executive Assistants can develop it too!

Let's demystify this concept and discuss how you can cultivate your executive presence and grow your career.

WHAT IS EXECUTIVE PRESENCE?

Executive presence, in short, is your ability to inspire confidence in your leader, your colleagues, and your direct reports. For EAs, this is especially important because you are often asked to lead without a traditional title of authority and must rely on your influential leadership skills to make things happen. Furthermore, you are leading up to your Executive and down and out to others throughout the organization. Executive presence is an amalgamation of confidence, poise, clear and concise communication, reliability, vulnerability, and strength. Quite the tall order, right?

WHY DO YOU NEED EXECUTIVE PRESENCE?

So why is executive presence important for Force Multipliers? Executive presence is all about access and opportunity. By inspiring confidence in your leader, you will get asked to take on higher-profile projects. By exuding executive presence, you will be a part of the decision-making process. Executive presence will allow you to command a seat at the table and be an invaluable strategic business partner and leader alongside your Executive.

HOW DO YOU BUILD EXECUTIVE PRESENCE?

Like any other skill, with time and intention, you can develop executive presence. Executive presence is essential for Executive Assistants and Force Multipliers as you interact with more leadership team members and executives than perhaps anyone else in the organization. How you show up sets the tone for your organization and, beyond that, for your career growth.

NINE WAYS FOR EXECUTIVE ASSISTANTS AND FORCE MULTIPLIERS TO DEVELOP EXECUTIVE PRESENCE:

1. **Develop your personal and professional vision.** Do you know what you want and where you are going? If not, take the time to figure that out and hone your "elevator pitch" for your career and your life. One tool we use is called Your Future Self. It allows you to really envision what you want your life

to look like in three years and then start manifesting that into reality by reading it daily. Share Your Future Self with your Executive, spouse, family, and friends. When you are clear on where you are going (and what you will say yes to and what you will say no to), you will earn the respect of everyone in your circle. Beyond that, it will give you the language to clearly articulate who you are, what you do, where you are going, and the impact you are making on the world, whether you're at a networking event, chatting with another EA, socializing at a family BBQ, or sharing the elevator with the Chairman of the Board.

2. **Strengthen your self-awareness.** Self-awareness is the cornerstone of success. It is the conscious knowledge of one's own character, feelings, motives, and desires. It's about knowing what you are good at and what you are not good at and owning it. Self-awareness is knowing how you show up at your best, how you communicate, how you receive information, and how you react when under stress. Taking behavior and personality assessments and really studying those traits can help you gain clarity about yourself and how you are perceived by others. Knowing when and how to adjust your communication style is all part of building executive presence.

3. **Cultivate exceptional communication skills.** A leader's three most important jobs are to cast the vision, provide clarity and direction, and remove roadblocks. A Force Multiplier's most important job is to help a leader accomplish those objectives, all of which can be boiled down to one thing: communication. Building great written and oral (in-person, on the phone, or via video) communication skills will set you apart.

4. **Develop confidence.** I know many EAs may hesitate to take on new projects and instead wait to be assigned tasks, but don't wait! In fact, Executives are looking to you to step up and take

things off their plates. If you are not confident in your own abilities, why would an Executive want to hand off important projects to you? Get uncomfortable, and be okay with failing forward. No one is perfect. In fact, if you don't take risks from time to time and push yourself, you are never going to fully realize what you are capable of. And each time you take on a project that you didn't quite think you were ready for or have that tough conversation with your Executive and realize that you were able to handle it, you gain a little more confidence. And then a little more. Confidence takes practice. Lean into the uncomfortable moments, and know that you can figure anything out. Your leader and your team will appreciate your willingness to try and your ability to get things done. That is executive presence.

5. **Own your failures and your successes.** As you begin to push the boundaries of what's comfortable, you're going to make mistakes. Own up to them immediately. Share what you learned or would do differently next time, and bring a solution and plan of action to fix it. Having executive presence doesn't mean that you get everything right. In fact, the best leaders are vulnerable and transparent when they make the wrong decision. It's the next step that sets the great leaders apart. Do they take ownership? And do they show strength and decisiveness on how they are going to fix it and move forward? As a Force Multiplier, you must do this too. Owning your failures is step one. Step two is being willing to own your successes, which—believe it or not—can sometimes be harder to do! I know Executive Assistants generally like to operate behind the scenes, but when a project comes together because of your efforts or the President thanks you for your work, do not deflect or downplay your contribution! Executive presence is the ability to sit with your failures and your successes and own them both.

6. **Learn to listen and ask great questions.** Some of the best communicators are the ones that listen and ask powerful questions. Executive presence means confidence. And confident individuals do not need to be the loudest or smartest in the room. In fact, if you're the smartest person in the room, you're probably in the wrong room! As an Executive Assistant, your ability to listen to your leader and ask questions that drive clarity for them and the rest of the organization is a critical skill. Influential leaders are masters at challenging someone's thinking, helping them to consider another perspective, or helping them self-discover a new way of doing something. Those are powerful people to have on your team. Be that person for your Executive.

7. **Manage your emotions.** No one understands chaos and crisis more than a leader and their Force Multiplier. How are you showing up when the stakes are high? People often attempt to appear busy and rushed to signify value to the organization. However, slow is smooth, and smooth is fast. Leaders with executive presence remain centered and are calm under pressure and deliberate and purposeful in their actions. Overwhelmed and flustered EAs do not inspire confidence in their leader. This is not to say that you should hide your frustrations or challenges (particularly from your Executive), but manage your emotions and communicate your challenges professionally, in a timely manner, and with a couple of ideas of how to move forward. Remember, you don't have to have all the answers, but you do need to be willing to have the conversation and work through it together.

8. **Build your leadership capital.** Leadership capital is similar to political capital in that it is the accumulation of resources and power built through relationships, trust, goodwill, and influence between various stakeholders. Leadership capital is

a finite (yet renewable) resource that must be used wisely and cultivated consistently. Executive Assistants can build their leadership capital by honing their job-specific skills (executive support, project management, logistics, etc.). From there it is all about relationships—maintaining loyalty to your leader, managing relationships between internal and external stakeholders, and helping your team members achieve their personal and professional goals. The third component is building your reputation by following through and following up, taking action, and doing what you said you were going to do (or ensuring your Executive's promises made are kept). Leadership capital is a big part of executive presence.

9. **Lead yourself first.** And finally, self-leadership precedes leadership. You must lead yourself first before anyone else will ever follow. Executive presence must start with your willingness to do the hard work to grow as a human and as a leader. Everything I mentioned above requires discipline, the purposeful pursuit of personal growth, and daily practice. If you don't even keep promises to yourself (waking up at 5:00 a.m., reading a book a week, finishing your MBA, or taking Friday afternoons off), then how can you expect your leader or your team members to have confidence in you? Leading yourself is the first step to building and maintaining your executive presence.

The good news is, executive presence is something you can develop over time with focused intention, as is leading up.

ACHIEVE MORE TOGETHER

- Complete a Your Future Self worksheet, and share it with your Executive/Executive Assistant.
- Create an Elevator Pitch.
- Do one thing this week that is outside of your comfort zone. Reflect on what went well and what you learned.
- Determine your one-minute recentering practice.
- During your next meeting or conversation, challenge yourself to only ask questions.
- Review the nine ways to develop executive presence. Choose one to work on this month. What action step can you take today to get you moving in the right direction?

LEADING UP

Working on your executive presence will help you develop the leadership skills and confidence you need to lead up. Leading your Executive is no different than leading any other project, except that you feel you have a lot more riding on the outcome. It could be your fear of making a mistake or of getting fired. It could be that you don't want to sound unintelligent so you hold back. Regardless, you've got to get over yourself. You need to play full-out as a leader if you really want to be taken seriously in your role. It may not always work out—you may lose your job if your Executive can't handle you—but that just means you will open yourself up to an opportunity to work with an Executive who can match your drive and assertiveness. I'll let you in on a little secret here: most successful leaders want a Force Multiplier who is willing to lead up. Leaders need to be led too!

WHAT DOES IT MEAN TO LEAD UP?

1. **Understand your Executive's goals.** Yes, you want to be in alignment with the mission and goals of the organization, but your primary responsibility is to support your Executive;

therefore, you need to first be aligned with his goals and vision (for his career, his division, and/or his business). Once you understand his goals, you can be proactive in searching for opportunities to further your Executive's agenda and help him get there.

2. **Challenge your Executive.** One key component of leading up is challenging your Executive's thinking, and what better way to do that than by asking questions that help them see a different perspective and strengthens their thinking? This goes beyond just playing devil's advocate, though that is a good start. I am very vocal about telling people that Hallie pisses me off almost daily because she challenges my thinking. Now, she's not just disagreeing or arguing for argument's sake. We can both argue either side of an issue. Bringing a different perspective or pointing out how a particular decision will affect our brand reputation or impact our staff members is valuable. Recently, I wanted to write a blog post offering commentary on the recent suicides of two pop culture icons. Hallie was not convinced the argument had a well-formulated angle, nor did she think either one of us had enough expertise to offer our opinions. She voiced this concern and offered both a different angle and a different topic altogether. We ultimately decided to go with a different topic that week. Bring awareness to a situation, ask powerful questions, and offer a solution. Then make a decision together and implement it.

3. **Provide sound advice.** News flash: your Executive doesn't know everything. He does look to you to be the eyes and ears of the organization, report back, and provide sound advice. This goes hand in hand with challenging your Executive. Make sure your arguments are well formulated, and arm yourself with the facts. Concrete numbers and solid evidence help you and your Executive make better decisions.

4. **Learn how your Executive thinks by asking powerful questions.** One of the most important parts of being a strong strategic partner and invaluable Force Multiplier is understanding how your leader or Executive thinks and makes decisions. While it would be nice to be able to read their mind, that's just not possible (yet). In lieu of mind-reading capabilities, you can get better at understanding your leader's decision-making process with some key practices and, of course, by asking really great questions. Why? Because it helps drive clarity in the conversation, prioritize projects, and, ultimately, understand not only why we are making a decision but who we will need to help execute it and how we're going to get it done. When Hallie and I have these conversations, she's learning how I think, how I make decisions, what information I am triangulating, how long I'm going to wait before moving ahead, and more. Your EA can help move that process along by having a series of questions at their fingertips. While your EA is helping to clarify points for the rest of the team, it also is an excellent way to help your Force Multiplier hone their leadership skills and learn how you think and make decisions so they can be one step ahead in the future.

5. **Anticipate your Executive's needs.** Understand the company's goals and your Executive's role in achieving them, and then look for any opportunity to enhance his work. Pay attention to what is consistently bogging down your Executive, and volunteer to take over those responsibilities. Know that your boss is always going to forget a pen and always needs coffee at 3:00 p.m. Make sure he is prepared with questions for his next podcast interview ten minutes prior to the call, not two days prior (because you know he never reviews anything that far in advance). Never let him be blindsided by an upset client or a canceled meeting. An Executive has a million things running

through his mind; you've got to be tactical and prepared to jump in to assist before he even knows what he needs, all while communicating to all parties every step of the way.

6. **Understand your Executive's natural behavior.** Study behavior and personality profiles, and learn what makes your boss tick. Understanding his core behavior will have a profound effect on how you interact and communicate with him—and ultimately lead him.

7. **Know how your Executive prefers to communicate.** Does he prefer email, phone, or text? Is there a certain time of day that is better? When is the best time to discuss a problem and bring a solution? How quickly does he expect a response? Knowing how your Executive prefers to communicate will help you guide him with projects and decisions. That's leading up.

8. **Teach your Executive how to work with you.** This means stepping up and asking for more responsibility and not being afraid to showcase your previous accomplishments or unique talents and skills. Your Executive has partnered with you to make his life easier; show him how you can do that!

9. **Respect your Executive's time.** Protect his time, even if that means protecting him from himself or from you! Learn when it is best to meet and collaborate with your Executive and when he just needs a minute alone. Just because you have a pile of work to get through does not mean that is a priority for him. He might just need a minute to get some water or call his wife! Getting a signature now might make your day easier, but that is not the way this relationship works.

Leading up doesn't just apply to your Executive. Executive Assistants must constantly be managing the expectations of their colleagues and leading everyone toward a common goal. For example, you probably know what your Executive means when he assigns you a task—he wants it done immediately, worst case by the end of the day (and you know exactly what "end of the day" means).

When you are working with other team members, if you are unsure of a deadline, you have to ask. Better yet, give *them* a deadline. Keep it aggressive but realistic. When you're given a new project by anyone other than your Executive, ask the requester when they need it completed by. If that works for you, knowing all the other projects you're working on, great. If it doesn't, make sure you communicate that and offer an alternative. If your team member says, "Whenever," suggest a time frame for when you can complete the task, and get their agreement. You must always be driving toward clarity. "Whenever" to your team member might mean two days, while "whenever" means two weeks to you.

Executive Assistants may also be called upon to lead other people in the office. While your primary responsibility is to your Executive, the company is a close second. Anything you can do to help the leadership team or other key company stakeholders accomplish their goals is ultimately helping the company and your Executive. Know the goals of your division or the leadership team, and check in with those team members to see how you can support them in their growth and goals.

By keeping your commitments, delivering projects before their deadlines, and keeping your boss and other stakeholders in the loop about the progress you've made on various projects, you are establishing yourself as a leader. The work you do is a direct reflection on your Executive. When you shine, your Executive shines, and that makes everyone happy.

Remember, leadership and leading up are an inside game. It always starts with you. Read on to learn more about how to lead yourself first.

> ### ACHIEVE MORE TOGETHER
>
> - Do you clearly understand your Executive's goals and how you can contribute to the results? If not, schedule a meeting to discuss today!
> - Force Multipliers, are you setting clear deadlines and expectations with your team members and coworkers? Do you hold your boundaries when they ask you for help? Why or why not? What are some alternative options?
> - Are you able to anticipate your leader's needs? If not, schedule a time to discuss ways you can better support your Executive, take notes, and follow through.
> - This week, recommend an article, book, podcast, etc., to your leader that you know is aligned with their vision and will help them reach their goals.

LEAD YOURSELF FIRST

Mastering the ability to lead up starts by leading yourself first. Executive Assistants should be working on their personal and professional growth intentionally. The more confidence you have in yourself, by working on your executive presence, leadership and communication skills, personal growth, and business acumen, the more that confidence is going to permeate all corners of the business and eventually reach the Executive, who won't be able to help but have confidence in you.

Remember, confidence doesn't mean you have all the answers or know everything. Confidence is knowing you can find a solution to any challenge that comes your way. Confidence is the cornerstone of leading yourself.

Leading yourself first means that you have both a personal and a career development plan in place. What are you learning about the industry? What conferences and seminars are you planning on attending each year? What books are you reading? Do you have specific responsibilities you want to take on? Are you taking a class to build a new skillset or get a certification? Share your career development plan with your Executive and team!

What about in your personal life? What are you doing to challenge yourself and get outside of your comfort zone? Are you registering for a marathon or a new dance class? Are you joining an improv group? Are you backpacking across Europe alone?

The best way to learn is by teaching others. To practice your leadership, host an administrative mastermind or teach a free seminar on a topic you're passionate about. Perhaps you need a coach to take your leadership to the next level. Get one.

Leading yourself means committing to growing, and committing to the necessary accountability to get there. Leading yourself is undoubtedly more challenging than leading others. Master this and you've set yourself up for long-term success.

Simply put, leadership is influence. Founders and Force Multipliers, it's your job to show the way by constantly learning, growing, and sharing your experiences along the way.

ACHIEVE MORE TOGETHER

- Create a Growth Plan
  - Outline your goals for the year.
  - Create actionable and measurable steps for your growth. What conferences will you attend? How many books will you read? What podcasts or master classes do you need to listen to? Do you need a certificate? Are you going to volunteer? How many days a week are you going to work out? What new projects or responsibilities do you want to take on at work? How many vacations do you plan to take? How do you plan to get out of your comfort zone? Do you mentor or coach someone? What fitness equipment do you need to buy? Who do you need to connect with more often?
  - Sign up for and schedule all of the above activities, events, deadlines, vacations, etc.
  - When they show up on your calendar, just do the activity! Your growth will be inevitable at that point.
- Share your Growth Plan with your Executive and vice versa so you can help hold each other accountable and keep growing together.

PART FOUR

TIME AND ENERGY MANAGEMENT

ADOPT A NEW MINDSET ABOUT TIME

You may not be able to buy happiness, but you can buy time, and in my book, that is just a hop, skip, and a jump from happiness and freedom! As a Founder & CEO (heck, as a human!) time is really all I have.

And we all have twenty-four hours in a day. So why do some people accomplish more than others? Look, you can't create more hours in the day (if you figure out how to do that, you'll be living the rich and famous life!). You can't shift time, and you really can't manage or control time. Time is not the cheat. Time is time. But what you can control and what you can manage is yourself. You can lead yourself to be the most effective that you can be within the time you have each day.

Most Entrepreneurs, business owners, and business leaders are driven by freedom. I know I am. Freedom is what drives every decision I make. Freedom is what gets me up at 4:30 a.m. and keeps me inspired all day. Financial freedom. Freedom to give by richly blessing other people's lives. Physical freedom. Spiritual freedom to truly understand and accept myself and others. Social freedom to experience the journey of life with other people when and where I choose. It's all about freedom. But when Executives move into leadership positions or start their own businesses, they can become intoxicated by the freedom of being their own boss and stop following any sort of structure—the structure that helped them become successful in the first place.

As an Entrepreneur, your secret weapon for leading and managing yourself, and therefore "managing" time, is your Executive Assistant. Not to mention—*if we're being honest*—how many things are Entrepreneurs and leaders really good at? Probably about three: creating and casting the vision, providing clarity and focus to the team, and making high-quality decisions to keep the company on track. That's it. The rest? Most Founders are going to delegate those tasks out as quickly as possible or just not do them at all.

Again, let's give thanks to all the Force Multipliers out there! They are a huge asset for helping leaders manage their time and energy.

FEELING TRAPPED

I remember feeling completely trapped when I first started working with Hallie. One of her core responsibilities was to manage my schedule, including scheduling appointments and generally telling me where to be and when. I hated it. Every time I saw a new meeting, I had a physical reaction of panic mixed with rage. I felt like my time was being taken from me. Didn't I become an Entrepreneur in the first place so I could do whatever I wanted? I quickly learned, though, that wasn't the case, and I started to make my schedule work in my favor. I began shifting my mindset from "My time is being taken and controlled" to a mindset of "I am in control of how I choose to invest my time." I realized that if I was going to be as successful as I wanted to be, I was going to have to make each minute count.

Within about a year, I had my schedule down to a science. I worked at the office from about 8:00 a.m. to 11:30 a.m. (and knew I had a break from 11:30 a.m. to 1:00 p.m. every day to clear my email, meditate, eat lunch, and do whatever the heck I wanted to!). No big deal. I could power through appointments from 8:00 to 11:30. I had another burst of work in the afternoon from 1:00 to 4:00. Then I would go home and spend time with my family before hopping back on email around 7:30 p.m., after the kids went to bed, for a last-minute check-in with the team.

It didn't happen overnight, but now I understand just how important it is to have discipline with my schedule and my time. Now, maintaining this discipline and controlling how I invest my time becomes increasingly difficult when you add in the fact that I have someone else handling that for me. This is why it is essential for EAs and Executives to be on the same page with goals and priorities (insert regular communication and meetings here). Executives must work closely with their Executive Assistants to ensure their time is being spent on only the most important activities and that the EA is protecting their personal time (working out, reading, family time, etc.) too.

SHIFT YOUR MINDSET AROUND TIME

First, let's check your mindset around time. Think about the last time someone asked you how you were doing. The standard response used to be "I'm fine." Now the response is almost always

"Busy!" It's like it's cool to be busy. But when I hear busy, I just think of a lot of meaningless activity. I think of someone going from one task to the other, undisciplined and haphazard. The question is, "Are you being productive?" Productive means you're using your time well, only focusing on the most important tasks, and saying no (or having your EA say no) to everything else.

Furthermore, if you're running around saying you don't have time for this or don't have time for that, then you are creating a scarcity mentality around time—and a self-fulfilling prophecy. If you argue for your limitations, you're going to get them. Keep telling yourself you don't have any time, and guess what. You won't. *Make* the time. Be conscious of the language you use around time.

Several years ago, we added a sign to the bottom of our employees' computers that says, "Am I being active, or am I being productive?" It's a focusing question that brings everyone back to thinking about how they are utilizing their time. It helps everyone think about whether what they are doing right then is actually helping their Executive, their team, or the company move forward. And if it's not, then they probably shouldn't be doing it! It's time to make a decision about whether that task could be delegated, rescheduled for a later date, or eliminated altogether. When you feel yourself going into that spiral of never having enough time, just stop— because all you are doing is perpetuating the cycle that there is never enough time to do what you need or want to do. The reality is, there is always enough time to get the most important things done (as long as you are extremely clear on what those things are).

In fact, there is a law about it. Parkinson's Law states, "Work expands so as to fill the time available for its completion." Remember that crash diet you went on four weeks before a beach vacation where you lost twenty-five pounds and looked smoking in your Speedo? Remember that pitch deck you created less than twenty-four hours before your meeting with a prominent investor? How about purchasing the perfect tenth-anniversary gift for your wife with minutes to spare? You couldn't seem to get yourself going before, but hell, with that deadline looming, you somehow did everything you needed to get done just in the nick of time. You didn't magically get more time; you just got the right clarity and motivation.

Remember, you only get done about 65 percent of what you had planned for the day or week. And that's okay. You just have to keep coming back to your top 20 percent and make sure you are accomplishing those major objectives. The rest is simply going to fall into place with the time you have left. If you were constantly trying to get everything on your to-do list done by the end of the day, you would never stop working. For Entrepreneurs and Executive Assistants, the work is truly endless. You must know when to stop, when to say no, and what is okay to leave until tomorrow.

ACHIEVE MORE TOGETHER

- Have you given up control of your calendar to your Executive Assistant? If not, now's the time!
- Force Multipliers, determine what type of communication your Executive needs in order to feel comfortable with you managing their calendar. Find out what days and times are off limits, and get their permission to schedule at your discretion within those guidelines.

TREAT EVERY WEEK LIKE YOU'RE GOING ON VACATION

There's nothing like an upcoming vacation to get your priorities straight and your ass in gear. Why is it that most of us are so much more productive and efficient leading up to a holiday or vacation? And how can we harness that productive power throughout the rest of the year? Simple. Take control of how you spend your time. That's why we're so purposeful before vacations. We prioritize like a boss. We only do what is most important, and we schedule our day down to the minute. I bet in the last day before a recent vacation you worked out, meditated, worked on your novel, put in a nine-hour day at the office (did three interviews, finished two projects, took the team out to lunch), went shopping for three new outfits, met your partner and some friends for dinner, spent another hour checking in with your team and answering emails, and read two chapters of *The Surrender Experiment*. Why isn't every day this purposeful and productive?

A looming vacation is a perfect example of Parkinson's Law. The key is translating this concept into your everyday life. The most successful people follow a schedule and have a rhythm to their days and weeks—from workouts to meetings to date nights to interviews to planning time. If it is not in your calendar and on your schedule, it isn't real, and it doesn't get done.

I'm going to talk directly to Executive Assistants here for a bit because the idea of extreme time management is even more critical, and a hell of a lot more complex, for Executive Assistants. They not only have to manage and maximize their Executive's time, but they must still make enough time in the day to work on other key projects to help move the company forward. My Executive Assistant and Hallie live in my calendar—it dictates the flow of my day and, therefore, to a certain degree, theirs. But in addition to preparing for and attending many of the meetings I am at, they also have several meetings of their own that need to happen, as well as projects that need their time and attention. I know all of the EAs reading this book can create a damn good schedule. The issue often lies in execution. How do you manage your time when your time is not your own?

MANAGE YOUR TIME

Let's take a look at your calendar and your Executive's calendar. Right now, take a minute, open it up, and see what you've got planned for the week. I bet your Executive's calendar is flawlessly organized—every minute of his personal and professional time accounted for. Can you say the same about your schedule? Are you making time for what's most important?

Your time is just as valuable as your Executive's. If you are just moving from one request to the next or just getting lost in your emails all day, you are likely not making any meaningful progress on special projects or spending any time thinking or planning for growth—both key components of being a strategic partner and Force Multiplier. To move from being reactive to being proactive, you must manage yourself and therefore your time.

TIME BLOCKING WITH THE WEEKLY EXECUTION PLAN

Time blocking is a popular method for scheduling your days and weeks. Put all events, meetings, projects, and priorities in your calendar, and stick to it. I know, I know. It's not always possible. One of the main reasons leaders and Force Multipliers love their careers is because each day is different. Sure, there is a rhythm to the week—standing meetings, weekly deliverables—but what was important at 8:00 a.m. on Monday may not be important by noon. Flexibility is critical for an Executive Assistant to survive and thrive. If you do have to miss a meeting with yourself (say, working on a new standard operating procedure), then make sure you replace that block of time in your calendar later in the week.

Because of the variability of the days and weeks, Hallie prefers to use a combination of time blocking and her Weekly Execution Plan to create her weekly schedule. For example, Hallie maps out her three to five most important items for the week. During our weekly one-to-one meeting, we discuss these objectives and adjust if needed. From there, Hallie will front-load those high-priority projects into her calendar for the week (with the goal of completing those projects by Wednesday), working around all of her various recurring meetings.

Brooke Castillo, in her podcast, *The Life Coach School,* put this concept into a simple term: proactivation. Proactivation is the opposite of procrastination. It is about setting aggressive deadlines for yourself and front-loading your days and weeks with the most important tasks. I get it; it is so much more satisfying to answer emails or check off random tasks from your to-do list, but I guarantee that will not help your Executive grow the business. Instead, focus on foundational items such as the two-hour recruiting session for a Director of Sales or a three-hour block of time for creating fresh content for the website. Accomplishing those tasks in the beginning of the week frees you up to handle all the challenges that you know are going to come your way. The external demands and frequent fires are never going to stop, but proactivation can help you eliminate stress by at least getting high priorities off your plate first.

STOP MULTITASKING

So many EAs pride themselves on multitasking, but we know multitasking is a myth—unless we are engaged in low-level activities like walking and talking on the phone or folding laundry and watching Netflix. Multitasking in the high-pressure business environment you work in? It's just not effective. About two and a half hours are lost every day to multitasking (i.e., switching back and forth between tasks). The wise Publilius Syrus said, "To do two things at once is to do neither." As much as possible, set up your day so that you are batching projects and tasks. Can you do all your calls in one hour? Can all travel arrangements be made in a two-hour window on a Tuesday? Can confirming appointments for the next week, along with the corresponding meeting prep, all be done on a Friday afternoon?

We all have twenty-four hours in a day (and we don't want to spend it all at the office, no matter how much we love our job). Why can some people accomplish more in one day than most accomplish in a week? Because they are committed to living a structured life, managing their time, and getting clear on their priorities. The paradox is that by doing so, you ultimately have more time and freedom.

GET CLEAR ON PRIORITIES

You know those people? The ones who appear to be productivity geniuses, who seem to have been gifted the "get shit done" gene from a higher power? Well, I'm sorry to break it to you, but they are not really that special. Which means that what they do, you can do too. No excuses.

Where these people have pulled away from the pack, though, is by learning to look at their work with a critical eye. They aren't spending hours making a laundry list of tasks that need to be checked off one by one in no real order. They know the most important things that need to be done, and they have no qualms about slashing anything that doesn't help them hit their goals or assigning a task to someone who is better equipped to handle it. No ego. Only results.

At the end of the day, it's about effectiveness and impact and how much value is created through the completion of an action item.

CREATE A NOT-TO-DO LIST

At some point in the career of both an Entrepreneur and an Executive Assistant, there is just going to be too much work to do for the number of team members you have. This means it's time for some leverage. The first step is understanding exactly what another person would do for you (usually that means taking something off the Executive's or EA's plate). If you are at this place in your business, do this: for the next two weeks, keep track of everything that you do that is not a dollar-producing activity (yes, for your EA too!) or anything that you absolutely hate doing or that is not really in your strength zone. Now, when you make this list, it doesn't mean you get to stop doing those tasks. It just serves as a good reminder of the noncritical, non-dollar-producing activities that someone else might be amazing at and might also love to do. That list then becomes the job description for the next hire for the business.

I like the Trash, Transfer, and Trim Method from the book *Clockwork: Design Your Business to Run Itself,* by Mike Michalowicz, to help you streamline your work and increase your impact:

1. **Trash:** Do you have something on your to-do list that just doesn't need to be there? Maybe it's a project that no longer fulfills the mission of your organization or an obligatory phone call or email that is three months overdue. Perhaps it is yet another birthday party for a second cousin's third nephew. It's choosing what to say no to, so you can say yes to the most important items. Saying yes to drinks after work is probably going to throw off your evening routine, so don't do it. If it's not necessary for the goals of the business, your life, or your family, trash it.

2. **Transfer:** The first question I ask myself when a new idea or

project crosses my desk is, "Who can do it?" I do not immediately assign the project or task to myself. In fact, that's my last resort. If there is someone better equipped to handle a task (and there probably is), transfer it. Often, this will be a download to your Executive Assistant, who will then further delegate the task if needed.

3. **Trim:** If the project or task is something that you absolutely must be involved with, trim it. Limit your time. Do you have to be in a content brainstorming meeting? Keep it at twenty minutes max. Do you have to attend a speaker series? Request to speak first. Then pack a punch with your fifteen-minute presentation, and slip out the back door. If you must be involved, trim it.

The Trash, Transfer, and Trim Method is an effective way to focus your efforts on only the most important tasks to maximize your time, while continuing to impact your organization and your overall life goals.

STREAMLINE YOUR MEETINGS

The Trash, Transfer, and Trim Method is especially effective for meetings. A *Harvard Business Review* article, "The Leader's Calendar," reported that a survey of CEOs found they had an average of thirty-seven meetings in any given week, taking up 72 percent of their total working time. That's just too many damn meetings! Very few meetings need to last longer than thirty minutes.

About a year ago, I went through my calendar with Hallie and eliminated several meetings, cut many back to fifteen minutes, and limited the rest to thirty minutes. An Executive should generally only be in decision-making meetings. The rest of your team, your

EA included, should handle any planning and most strategy meetings. Once you are in the room, your team should present options in order for you to ask questions and make a decision.

In fact, most status updates and check-ins can be done via phone or email. If the content of a meeting could be just as effective in an email, send the email. A meeting is not necessary just to give an update. The best use of a meeting is to facilitate conversation and exchange ideas to make a decision, assign tasks, and then get to work implementing them.

Work with your Executive Assistant to identify who needs to be in what meetings. Be conscious of the two-pizza rule. If two pizzas aren't enough to feed the people in the room, there are too many people in the meeting. Meetings become inefficient and ineffective when there are fifteen-plus people in the room. A few years ago, during our ruthless elimination of meetings, we also recalibrated who needed to be in the room and took one meeting from twelve people down to seven. The meeting was cut down to about fifteen minutes. And focus and productivity increased.

After any meeting that you're in, spend five minutes (or less if your EA was in the meeting with you) doing a quick debrief. Are there any action items that need to be handled, information that needs to be gathered, or anyone who needs to be followed up with? Communicate that with your EA, and then she'll be on her way to force multiply on your behalf while you're on to your next meeting.

ACHIEVE MORE TOGETHER

- Review your calendars. Yes, right now. I know you can access it on your phone, which is sitting right next to you.
- What meetings on your calendar could actually be emails?
- Work together to eliminate any nonessential meetings. Can any of your current meetings be led by someone else? What's left? Cut all other meetings in half.
- Review your meetings and make sure the right people (and not too many people) are in each one.

IT'S OKAY TO BE SELFISH

Speaking of getting clear on priorities, I am unapologetically selfish with my time. I'll never forget some of the feedback I got after teaching my one-day seminar, "Limitless: Personal Growth Through Business Success." An attendee (anonymously) wrote, "[Adam] provided more information than needed about his personal life. His strict schedule…lucky kids get ten minutes a day of Dad's attention."

The funny thing is, the very issue that person noticed in that class was exactly what I get asked to speak about all around the country. I do have a strict schedule. So if being "selfish" is the antithesis to mediocrity, then I'm down.

In fact, I want every one of you reading this book to be more selfish with your time, relationships, goals, dreams, and desires. Being selfish actually allows you more room to grow and more room to give. While I know it sounds counterintuitive, believe me—it's not. Sure, you could be the "nice guy" who attends every five-year-old's birthday party with your kids. But will that really make an impact on your family's life, on your company, or on the lives of your employees or friends? Nope. Not even close. Be the selfish guy who passes on the party with a bunch of other children, and instead, spend that time engaging one-to-one with your own! Or pass on the party and reach out to an employee who needs coaching on the next phase of their career. Which one do you think has a bigger long-term impact? Yeah. Selfish doesn't sound so bad anymore, does it?

Have I been accused of being selfish? Of course I have. But when others try to put me down by calling me names, it's really just a reflection of their own insecurities and lack of discipline. I haven't built the business I have by catering to everyone else's agenda. I am not able to employ over 700 people around the country by being on someone else's schedule. I did not qualify for the 70.3 Ironman World Championship in South Africa with less than a year of training by saying yes to every social invitation. I put my personal and spiritual growth first. Period. Being "selfish" creates a strong foundation for your business and your life. By focusing on your growth first, you are able to be the best friend, partner, father, and leader possible.

Sounds great, right? To hell with anyone else! Well, it's not quite as easy as that. This is where you need to enlist your Executive Assistant to put this concept into action. Furthermore, you need to train and empower your assistant to just say *no*!

SAYING NO

Start saying no by making yourself less available. These open-door policies are putting a damper on productivity. I don't care if you are the CEO, assistant, sales associate, cleaning staff, or marketing director; your time is valuable. You have a job to do—for the company, yes, but ultimately what you do for the company should fulfill your personal goals and objectives too. When your office or cubicle has a revolving door, how much work are you actually getting done? When you say yes and allow yourself to be interrupted and distracted constantly, you are devaluing your time.

Close that revolving door, and instead schedule time for distractions. This can look like a thirty-minute block of time where you walk around the office and catch up with your staff. Perhaps you schedule "office hours" once a week where your team can hop on a Zoom meeting to chat, share a story, or ask for your advice. Regularly scheduled team meetings also cut down on the random questions and requests. Get standing meetings on your calendar that you can plan for and plan around.

Often open-door policies are used by staff to simply distract themselves from their work. They are procrastinating and looking for a distraction, and your open door is an open invitation to waste their time and yours. When you put these boundaries in place, you'll be surprised how the requests to "pick your brain" and ask questions drastically decrease. In fact, you'll actually be training your team to be more resourceful and self-sufficient because instead of coming to you for the answer, they will find it on their own. Role-model the behavior that your time is valuable and that discipline equals freedom, and your team members will follow. Increased productivity and more self-sufficiency for all.

If you are getting requests and invites that do not align with your ultimate life goals, just say no! No one is making you accept these offers. They all seem fantastic in the moment, but every time you say yes to something that doesn't align with your goals, you are saying no to your future results. Here's an example: when you say no to lead-generating for new clients and instead help a fellow colleague with the new team software, you're not in alignment with your goals. You may tell yourself you're being helpful, you don't want to be seen as a jerk, you want them to succeed. All of those may be true, but what about your success, your future, your family?

I don't know about you, but I respect the hell out of those individuals who can just say no with clarity and decisiveness. To me, it signals that they know exactly what they want and what their priorities are. And who can argue with that?

You have to help yourself first before you can help others. I hereby give you permission to be selfish! In the end, when you are disciplined with your time, you'll be able to make a bigger impact on those around you.

ACHIEVE MORE TOGETHER

- How can you be more selfish with your time, relationships, goals, dreams, and desires?
- What can you start saying no to this week?
- Executive Assistants, how can you help your leader be more strict and selfish with their time?

CREATE YOUR IDEAL
DAILY SCHEDULE

Have you picked up on the fact that living a scheduled, disciplined life is ultimately going to lead you to the results you want? Good. The next step is to create an ideal daily schedule to follow.

Creating an ideal daily schedule starts with working on the big picture—the annual items—and then you can fill in the monthly, weekly, and daily schedule. An Executive and EA must work on this together. Sure, the tactical part is that your EA needs to make sure everything is scheduled, but I encourage you to get more strategic than that.

For example, you may determine it's best if your EA takes vacations at the same time you do so she is able to more fully disconnect and isn't bombarded with emails and requests from you. Conversely, you may want your EA to be at the office while you're out of town, so the two of you need to plan vacations and travel accordingly. After your vacations and any training events or conferences are planned for the year (again, you may want your EA to travel to these events with you), then it's time to set the rhythm for the business. This includes weekly one-to-one meetings, monthly team meetings, quarterly off-sites, annual company events, and more. Finally, get granular about your daily schedule.

An Executive and EA working on this together will help give the Executive some semblance of control and make him feel like he has at least some basic input into how his life will be organized for the year ahead. From there, the EA will be empowered to make day-to-day decisions autonomously, while keeping the Executive's preferences and priorities in mind at all times.

Here's what a typical day looks like for me:

A DAY IN THE LIFE OF ADAM
4:30 A.M.

Wake up and immediately drink a glass of water and go outside for a few deep breaths of fresh air (yes, even when it's -10 and snowing or when it's humid and 95. The point is to shock the system and move quickly into a different state). Sometimes I even go out barefoot in the snow to really feel alive!

4:40 A.M.

Meditate for twenty minutes. I have been practicing Transcendental Meditation® for the past eight years or so.

5:00 A.M.

I grab a cup of black coffee (French roast) and usually a seltzer (black cherry) and get settled into my focused journaling, thinking, and planning time.

5:05 A.M.

I have several different journals I write in each day. I use Evernote to journal. My journals include:

1. **Life Journal:** This is a stream of consciousness where I write about my life, my thoughts, my challenges, my successes—the good, the bad, and the ugly. I also reflect on where I focused my time on the day before, where I failed, and what went well. I do a quick check-in with myself about how I want to feel today and whether or not I am being responsible for my peace today. I also write out my priorities for the day.
2. **Gratitude Journal:** I write everything I am grateful for, usually seventy to one hundred things that come to mind. I just keep it flowing.
3. **Journal for My Wife:** Every day I write something different about her that I am grateful for. I also journal about what she is doing and how she is growing, and I include photos.
4. **Journal for My Kids:** Each child (I have two girls and a boy) has a separate journal, and I write something about each of them—something new they learned, a milestone, a moment we shared, etc. I also pull in photos and add them to the journal. This is really my way of recording everything they say and do (which is usually the funniest part!) so that we have a history of their lives.

I also review my Future Self, which gets delivered to my inbox every morning.

I quickly check emails and set the course for the day for my company. I usually send out a few emails touching base with my leadership team and share any ideas or items that need attention. I also answer any questions they may have so that I don't create a roadblock for them to get a project done.

6:00 A.M.

Work out for about an hour. I either go for a run or a bike ride, or I work out via Tonal.

7:15 A.M.

We have a long driveway, so every morning, Sarah (my wife) and I walk the kids to the bus stop. It's about a seven-minute walk down our driveway, and five or so minutes sitting with them at the end of the road, but it's some of the best minutes of the day. It's a great time to chat with them about the day ahead and listen to their thoughts, fears, or what they're excited about. We talk. We're engaged. We're moving. We're outside. I love this time.

Sarah and I walk home together, talking about kids, the day, life... it's really purposeful time with her too. Typically, that conversation leads into a ten- to fifteen-minute conversation back at the house. It's quiet and wonderful. Sarah makes me a smoothie every day for breakfast, usually some combination of greens, veggies, fruit, and a scoop of Vega protein.

8:15 A.M.

I usually leave for the office between 8:00 and 8:15, depending on the day. I listen to Audible (right now, *The Almanack of Naval Ravikant*) or sometimes rock out to music and sing loudly! I turn up the music loud enough so I don't have to hear myself sing. My kids are obsessed with "The Comeback" by the Zac Brown Band right now, and they got me listening to it too!

8:30 A.M.

Arrive at the office, grab a seltzer, and finish up any emails. I like a clean inbox. Review any meeting or presentation prep for the day ahead. Review and sign anything left on my desk from the night before that may need my signature.

9:00 A.M.

Record an episode for the *Business Meets Spirituality* podcast about the trends that leaders will need to be aware of and act on in the year ahead.

10:00 A.M.

Call with the CEO of another company to discuss organizational design and how to begin scaling.

11:00 A.M.

Call with the Chairman of the Board and leadership team of another company to discuss moving ahead on a joint venture deal.

11:30 A.M.

This is my free period. I have about an hour and a half most days, and I spend that time making phone calls to check in on personal items (for example, finishing some projects at my house), check email, eat lunch (Ezekiel bread topped with a spicy black bean burger, tomato, avocado, and a side of seltzer water), and then meditate for twenty minutes before I jump back into another burst of work in the afternoon. I also answer random calls and texts throughout the entire day in little pockets of time between meetings.

1:00 P.M.

Conduct a group coaching and training call for our Project | U participants.

2:00 P.M.

Call with the CEO and Co-Founder of a prop tech company to explore potential collaborations.

2:30 P.M.

Meeting with the head of the international real estate division was canceled. I pop out of my office for a few and go over some items with my Executive Assistant and Chief of Staff, and then I grab a seltzer and answer as many emails as I can.

3:00 P.M.

Consultation call with potential future real estate partners.

4:00 P.M.

Call with a venture capitalist to discuss the next steps to monetize and bring our SaaS to market.

4:30 P.M.

Quick cleanup of my inbox and head home. On the fifteen minute commute, I call my mom and then my dad. I make it a point to speak with them every day because you just never know when the last day might be.

4:45 P.M.—5:30 P.M.

Grab a snack of veggies and hummus and check-in with Sarah and the kids.

5:30 P.M.–6:00 P.M.*

*Depending on the day, I may work until 5:30 p.m. or 6:00 p.m. finishing up calls or responding to emails. This is not the norm, and I don't think it will be long term, but it is simply the season of business that I am in right now. My kids are also in activities until about 5:30 p.m. most days, so we all get home right around the same time.

5:30 P.M.

Evening family time begins! We have dinner, play, snuggle, deal with the kids fighting—you know, all that fun stuff! I put my phone in a drawer (85 percent of the time) so I can be present with my family. I do this until I feel like our "present" time is over. Sometimes that's because the kids have chosen a solo activity or because they are on their tablets (they have one hour a day to use them). During that time, I may jump back into my email, or I may not. If we're engaged in a game, in the hot tub, wrestling, or playing hide-and-seek, then I may not pull back out of my time with them. But I pay attention to the energy and their needs, which is the general rhythm of the night for us.

7:45 P.M.

We start the bedtime routine for the kids, which can take anywhere from thirty minutes to two hours.

9:00 P.M.

I'm usually asleep by 9:00. I am a big believer in the power of seven to nine hours of sleep a night, and I have optimized my sleep environment to make sure that no matter how many hours I get, they are quality hours. Some of my sleep "tools" include the ChiliSleep Ooler Sleep System, a fan, a vibrating mattress, and the Whoop app. I like to be purposeful and present when I sleep too!

IDEAL DAILY SCHEDULE FOR THE EXECUTIVE ASSISTANT

Once the Executive has nailed down his ideal daily schedule, then it's time for the Executive Assistant to work on hers. Okay, so it might not be exactly ideal, since it is based on someone else's schedule, but that is the nature of the beast. Make it as ideal as you can within the construct of your Executive's ideal schedule.

Do you like to get into the office early? Do you like to work from home? Are you a night owl? Do you like to eat at your desk or take an hourlong lunch? Do you want to leave early on Thursdays and work Saturday mornings instead? If you're unsure of how your preferences will work in conjunction with those of your Executive, just ask! It truly doesn't hurt to broach the subject, and you may be surprised how flexible your Executive will be (particularly if he is an Entrepreneur).

Once you have the basic structure of your day done, it's time to block out the bigger commitments on your calendar. Think: your sister's wedding, a vacation to Bora Bora, a long weekend in Napa, as well as every training event and conference you'll be attending during the year—whether with your Executive or solo.

Next, work through any regularly scheduled weekly, monthly,

quarterly, and annual meetings and conference calls (this makes up the majority of Hallie's and my week). From there, if you have regular responsibilities, block off time to complete those each week or month. For example, each week you may need to confirm all of your Executive's meetings and prep for those appointments. Perhaps you pull various financial or staffing reports for your Executive monthly. Or you may update his social media profiles quarterly but check all of his profiles for messages daily. Put all of those recurring tasks on your calendar. Then, each week when you are going over that week's objectives with your Executive, make sure you block off time to complete any new or high-priority projects throughout the week (these will usually need to be done in blocks of two to three hours). Remember, front-load those in your day or week!

I've said it before, and I'll say it again: making sure you and your Executive stick to your scheduled time together is so critical. That is, hands down, the most important meeting of the week for both of you. It sets the tone for your Executive, for you, and for the organization. Make sure you clearly understand that week's three to five objectives, because they often change week to week, especially in a startup or high-growth company.

Once you have a cadence to your days, weeks, and months, it's imperative that you maintain that schedule, adjusting when necessary yet always pushing forward. If you have to erase a time block for whatever reason, make sure you replace it somewhere later in your week so you stay on track for your weekly, monthly, and quarterly goals.

Let's talk specifics. How are you starting off your day at the office? How you spend your first fifteen minutes sets the tone for the entire day. Do you make a beeline for your office and immediately get through as many emails as possible? Have you prepared a project the night before so you can dive into a three-hour time block? Do you check in with your Executive? Do you like to grab coffee and make your rounds of the office? There is really no right or wrong answer. Just make sure that whatever activity you choose is best serving you, your Executive, and the top 20 percent of your responsibilities.

For some of you, your calendar may be identical to your Executive's. Perhaps it is necessary to be at every meeting he's at to listen in, learn, take notes, and follow up. If that is the case, your day may be extended for several hours simply because when you are in meetings with him all day, you have little time for follow-up or prepping for the next day. I do think it's very important, especially in the beginning when you are learning about both your Executive and your company, to sit in on everything that you can. Eventually, you may be able to eliminate some of these meetings and only sit in on the most mission-critical meetings. Instead of participating in each one, perhaps you build into your Executive's calendar a five-minute debrief after each meeting so your Executive can quickly download any action items.

The following is an example of Hallie's daily schedule as Chief of Staff:

HALLIE NARRATES: A DAY IN THE LIFE OF HALLIE

5:00 a.m.

Alarm goes off. Enzo and Stella, our golden retriever/chow mix pups, jump into bed. I hit snooze and often drift back to sleep for fifteen minutes. At 5:15 a.m., I scan through my emails and social media messages and notifications, taking care of anything urgent or that can be answered quickly. Mostly I'm just looking for what new items might be on tap for the day that I didn't know about before I went to bed the night before.

5:30 a.m.

By this time I am out of bed, opening my laptop, drinking my pre-workout drink, and pulling up my workout video for the day while I knock out a few more emails.

6:00 a.m.

Throw in a load of laundry and work out in my home gym with Beach-body on Demand. I'm usually doing a program that consists of weights, HIIT, boxing, and/or mobility.

6:45 a.m.

Drink a smoothie (vanilla rice protein powder, spinach, oat milk, and frozen bananas). Get ready for the day while listening to a book on Audible or a podcast. Scan and answer emails as they come in.

8:00 a.m.

Pour some cold brew coffee into my Yeti and hop into the car for my twenty-minute commute to the office, listening to Audible (currently *Measure What Matters* by John Doerr). I always have a business or personal development book, memoir, biography, or autobiography to listen to.

8:30 a.m.

Check emails. Finish up any last-minute prep for Adam or myself for the day. Sign or review anything left on my desk from the night before.

9:00 a.m.

Weekly one-to-one meeting with Adam.

9:30 a.m.

Two screening interviews for the position of COO at our construction management and development company.

10:30 a.m.

Weekly one-to-one meeting with our Executive Assistant.

11:00 a.m.

Weekly one-to-one meeting with Marketing Manager.

11:30 a.m.–12:15 p.m.

Check emails. Finish writing an article. Connect with potential guests for *Business Meets Spirituality* podcast. Post a question or interesting article on LinkedIn to start a conversation.

12:15 p.m.

Adam pops his head into my office to talk briefly about a new potential business partnership. We discuss the pros and cons and I ask several clarifying questions. I tell him I will be doing some more due diligence and will map out some strategy and we'll revisit on Thursday morning.

12:30 p.m.

Eat lunch at my desk while reviewing emails or other work that team members need my feedback on. Call my husband.

1:00 p.m.

Weekly one-to-one meeting with CFO.

1:30 p.m.

Check emails and send out any follow-up or action items from morning meetings.

2:00 p.m.

With Adam gone on a business trip, I facilitate our weekly WIG (Wildly Important Goal) leadership meeting. I send the team's WIGs to Adam to keep him in the loop.

2:15 p.m.

Call with Event Manager at The Lodge at Spruce Peak to finalize details for our upcoming Project | U retreat. Go over last-minute action items with our Executive Assistant. Finalize agenda, content, and event program for Adam.

3:00 p.m.

Two calls with potential affiliate program partners for The Founder & The Force Multiplier. After the calls, I send them additional information, and we schedule a follow-up meeting for three weeks out.

4:00 p.m.

Consulting call with an Entrepreneur looking for counsel on how to correctly staff and organize his business and how to best work with his Executive Assistant.

4:30 p.m.

Call with the events team and host for an upcoming speaking engagement Adam will be conducting. We finalize the agenda and the specific topic Adam will be speaking on and go over last-minute logistics.

5:00 p.m.

Check email. Review my Weekly Execution Plan and to-do list and write out my to-do list for the following day.

5:30 p.m.

On the twenty-minute drive home, I call my husband quickly. I also call my mom. Then, I go back to listening to Audible.

6:00 p.m.

Make dinner with my husband and sit on the back deck with a glass of red wine while we catch up on our days and make plans for the weekend.

7:30 p.m.

Pick up the house, prep lunch for the next day, and head to my home office to check email and engage on social media, while watching the latest episode of *Summer House*.

8:30 p.m.

Walk the dogs. Get ready for bed. Unwind with a page-turning fiction book.

9:30 p.m.

Set my sleep timer on Audible for ten minutes and fall asleep.

Up next, I will share strategies for an Executive Assistant to streamline and manage their Executive's schedule. Better me than Adam!

ACHIEVE MORE TOGETHER

- Create your ideal daily calendars. Review them together. Make adjustments as needed.
- Determine how you are going to spend the first hour of your day and the first fifteen minutes of your workday.

22

HOW TO MANAGE YOUR EXECUTIVE'S TIME

**HALLIE NARRATES: HOW TO MANAGE
YOUR EXECUTIVE'S TIME**

With great power comes great responsibility. Once the ideal daily schedule is created, you will not only be responsible for organizing your Executive's day, week, and year, but you will also help determine who gets in to see your Executive and when. Use your power for good! Be solution-based and accommodating whenever possible.

Adam gets several meeting requests each day from people who want to take him to lunch, sell him their new product, or go to coffee and "pick his brain." At this point in my career, I can pretty easily tell which opportunities he'll be interested in and which ones he won't (e.g., anything involving a lunch or "brain picking" is a no). However, depending on who requests the meeting or if I think the product or service might be something we would be interested in, I offer an alternative. These requests are never met with a hard no, but rather with another option. Adam is not always the best person to meet with, so I connect the individual with the best person (many times, that is me, and I will take the meeting on Adam's behalf). If it is simply something we are not interested in and they will not take a meeting with another team member, I will let them know that they can follow up at a later date (and then we'll just do the same thing again if necessary). Then the ball is in their court to follow up, and I can take it off my plate and off my mind.

Schedule Decision-Making Meetings

As Adam mentioned, your Executive should only be in decision-making meetings. It's important for the Executive Assistant to be in on the planning meetings—to make sure all parties understand the Executive's objective and scope of work, to offer her Executive's perspective, and to help guide the discussion to ensure the team is moving in the right direction. Once the team has had time to work through the various pieces, weigh all options, create a budget, and analyze the ROI, then it's time to schedule a meeting for the team with the Executive where the two or three options can be presented for a decision. This saves a significant amount of time for your Executive and is just one example of why it's so critical for an EA to understand her Executive's goals.

Manage Deadlines

When managing your Executive's time, it's also important to be aware of deadlines and to manage the pieces leading up to the deadline accordingly. Set smaller, proactive deadlines along the way in order to ensure that the entire project is complete or talking points are organized prior to a client meeting.

Create Themed Days

Another strategy that has worked well for us is creating themed days whenever possible. This is just another form of time blocking or batching your Executive's work. Can you get all company meetings into one day? Can all coaching calls be stacked into a three-hour window on a Wednesday? Perhaps Thursdays are reserved for interviews (whether that's being interviewed for a podcast or article or interviewing potential leadership candidates). The more you can keep similar types of meetings together, the less time it takes for you to prepare and the more streamlined your Executive's day will be. Not to mention, the less mental energy it will take to constantly be switching between types of meetings or projects. While your Executive is safely ensconced on Zoom for three hours, that also allows you concentrated time to work on one of your priority projects. Win-win.

Maximize Travel Time

In addition, streamline and maximize productivity (and personal fulfillment) during the Executive's travel time. If he can take calls while traveling, great. Perhaps it makes sense for you to travel to the airport with your Executive and get all of your questions answered for the week before sending him off on vacation with his family. If your Executive is training for a marathon or doesn't want to interrupt his yoga practice, make sure you schedule those activities into his personal or business travel. When he's traveling, keep an eye out for an activity he might want to indulge in. For example, if he's traveling to California and he loves wine, ask if he would like to tour a vineyard after his business meeting. In addition, encourage him to take his family on business trips as much as possible. Maximize his time out of the office because it is critical for your Executive to enjoy a full life. The more you can facilitate that, the better!

Protect the Executive's Time

I can't emphasize enough how important it is to not overschedule your

Executive. Make sure he has space in his day to think, eat, or just go to the bathroom! If he likes to prep before meetings or reflect after them, then make sure you build in some white space between meetings. He may prefer to work in bursts, like Adam does, so schedule your Executive for two to three hours of back-to-back commitments, and then make sure he has a two-hour break in the middle of his day before going into the second burst of meetings.

Also, never let your Executive miss a personal commitment! Entrepreneurs and leaders work hard. They make a lot of sacrifices, many of which affect their personal life and relationships. Do not contribute to the problem, but rather be the catalyst for good. Make sure you have every date night, school play, parent-teacher conference, coffee with Mom, soccer game, and birthday and anniversary on the calendar. Offer suggestions for restaurants or gifts to make the most of these moments for your Executive and his family.

When managing your Executive's time, make sure you protect whatever time is sacred to him. For Adam, exercise, meditation, journaling, and family time are nonnegotiable. Find out what that is for your Executive, and protect it like a mother.

Do a Weekly Calendar Review

Each week, review the calendar with your Executive. Every Sunday night, Adam reviews the week ahead and eliminates any meetings that are not mission-critical. Often, we've scheduled meetings months in advance, and as a fast-growing company, what was important two months ago just may not be the best use of our time now. We don't necessarily cancel those meetings, but I will either take the meeting on Adam's behalf, or we will reschedule for a later date. Because most Executives live and die by their calendar, make sure you are reviewing it regularly to ensure the right things are on the calendar, and make adjustments as needed. Nobody wants their time wasted, especially not your Executive.

Direct Traffic

Confirm all meetings for the week ahead (preferably on a Thursday or Friday). This pertains to internal meetings as well. Review the schedule, and make sure all external appointments are confirmed and that both the attendee and the Executive have all relevant information. For internal meetings, make sure your team members are prepared to bring pertinent information to the meeting with your Executive so that it is a decision-making meeting. Perhaps there have been updates to the priorities that week or a new development. It is your responsibility to relay this information to your coworkers so that they don't waste their time or your Executive's time. If meetings need to be canceled or rescheduled, make sure everyone knows. If your Executive is running late, communicate that information. You are the traffic director and must keep the communication, people, and projects moving in the right direction at all times.

Keeping your Executive on schedule comes with a few caveats. It's your job to keep your eye on the calendar and on the clock. If he is running a few minutes over in a meeting, you've got to interrupt so that the entire day isn't derailed. However, this is where your judgment and knowledge of the business and overall company objectives come into play. It may be perfectly fine for your Executive to spend ten extra minutes with a potential investor or with a team member who is going through a particularly difficult time. If it's someone your Executive meets with every week, it may make sense to end the meeting right on time to make sure he's on time for his training webinar. It may be perfectly fine if your Executive is a few minutes late to an interview because he's finishing up a development deal. Each situation will be a bit different, so keep your eyes and ears open, and understand what is going on in the company.

As easy as it would be to operate solely by the book (therefore eliminating any guesswork about your Executive's schedule), that's just not the way business works. Know what is important to him, and keep the train moving along, on time as much as possible. Remind him of his next commitment. You wouldn't want him to be late for a family commitment because he was stopped in the hall by someone who wanted to get his thoughts on some random issue. Be the bad guy. Interrupt. Rescue your Executive. Do whatever you need to do to fulfill your Executive's commitments based on your judgment and discretion.

The key is making sure you over-communicate what is going on (while maintaining strict confidentiality) in order to maintain your Executive's reputation. Executives have many competing priorities and demands. It is the EA's job to communicate with all parties, to keep your Executive on time as much as possible, and, most importantly, to know when it's okay to make adjustments to the schedule. Being on the same page with your Executive and building that relationship of trust is critical to success.

Own the Schedule

As the keeper of your Executive's schedule, make sure everything that ends up on his calendar goes through you first, whether that is requests from employees, candidates, or the media; speaking opportunities; or personal commitments. Every calendar item should have complete information, including location, who will be at the meeting, topic of discussion, notes about attendees, travel time, call-in information, and more. If you, your Executive, or other people in your organization are adding meetings or sending calendar invites, then you may not be as prepared as you need to be for a meeting or may inadvertently offer that time to someone, not knowing that it's already scheduled. This takes time, but you and your Executive can train people to go to you. The Executive can simply reply to invitations, CCing the EA, and let the person who requested the meeting know that the EA will find a time in the next two weeks. Eventually, all requests will start going directly to the EA.

Effectively managing your Executive's time comes down to understanding the objectives of the organization, analyzing his schedule and commitments, strategically streamlining his days, and protecting his time. This is not a one-and-done activity. Time is the most important resource for both you and your Executive. Every quarter, review your Executive's calendar from a 30,000-foot view, and make adjustments as needed. Frequent minor adjustments will continue to keep your Executive's ideal daily schedule.

ELIMINATE WEAPONS OF MASS DISTRACTION

Having an ideal schedule is great. But we know that our days are not always going to go as planned.

You know it when you see it. You can probably spot it a mile away, coming down the hall, disguised as a pleasant conversation, an innocent question, or an innocuous request. But it's not harmless. It's not innocent—it's a weapon of mass distraction. Whether you see it coming or not, you are unable to stop it. Before you know it, your day is derailed, you are helping someone else with their work, or you've committed to another event that you didn't intend to commit to. What happened? Are you a pushover, a people-pleaser, an overachiever? (Note, I did not say high achiever!) Are you not in control of your time, your day, your words, and your life?

I'm not the only one who has struggled with this. Thankfully, I learned how to eliminate distractions years ago. It's going to happen to you again and again if you don't learn how to combat weapons of mass distraction. Every person in your organization (yourself included)—really, any person in your life—is hit with weapons of mass distraction daily, sometimes hourly. If you don't learn how to defuse these weapons, you can spin out of control, and before you know it, you will be fulfilling other people's needs and agendas and living someone else's life altogether. That is no way to live.

If you want people to respect your time and limit the weapons of mass distraction that they throw your way, the first step is to make sure you don't deploy weapons of mass distraction on others! Everyone's time is valuable in one way or another. Recognize that your emergency isn't necessarily someone else's emergency. Plan ahead. Give people lead time, clear direction, and accurate deadlines. Show up to meetings on time, stick to the agenda, and finish on time (early if possible!). When you respect your time and respect other people's time, they will respect yours, and maybe, just maybe, they'll begin to respect their own time as well.

Hallie is going to share why this is especially true for Executive Assistants.

HALLIE NARRATES: MANAGING INTERRUPTIONS

Unfortunately, one of the downsides of being an EA is that people don't always respect your time. They think you are there to serve their needs, pick up the pieces, and deal with whatever comes your way (yes, I know you *can*, but that doesn't mean you always *should*). EAs must stand up for themselves and protect their time, as well as that of their Executives. A critical aspect of time management is saying no. I was very much guilty of always saying yes and handling any request that came my way for many years, but I have learned that this is actually a disservice to myself, to Adam, and to the growth of the company. There is probably someone else on your team or on staff who can handle the request or project better than you can (I know—it's hard to believe, right?). Your job is simply to communicate the request to the appropriate person and then follow up (or better yet, ask that they follow up with you) so you know it was handled. Done. Move on to the priorities and projects that only you can handle.

It's about reclaiming your role and proclaiming that your time is just as valuable as anybody else's in the office. For you to be as effective as possible in your role and to be invaluable to your Executive (who is your primary focus), you've got to mitigate distractions and take a stand. It's a difficult thing to do, but you have to take control over your day and protect your time.

For example, if a request is going to take longer than sixty seconds to answer or requires research, sending additional documents, or bringing someone else into the conversation, then I always ask the person who is making the request to send me an email with exactly what they need, and I set a deadline for when I will handle it (say, within twenty-four hours). This does a few things. First, it puts the ball in their court to actually send the email (you'd be surprised how many people figure things out for themselves if you don't do it for them right away). Second, it allows you to maintain control over your day and handle that request during your time block for handling miscellaneous (non-Executive) requests. When you're an EA, people know that you know everything and are a badass at getting things done. By putting the onus back on them to make the request, you are leading up from every angle.

Remember: "No." Is a Complete Sentence

Learn how to say, "No, and..." All right, I'm not advocating for saying no to your Executive—unless it is to remind him that what he wants to do is not actually one of the critical objectives for the quarter. Part of our jobs as EAs is to figure out how to make stuff happen, but not at the expense of providing sound advice and reminding our Executives of the overarching goals. It may not be an outright no, but could be a suggestion to put a hold on the new idea and revisit it in a month.

This extends to the internal and external stakeholders that are constantly making requests of you and your Executive. For example, if someone asks Adam to speak at an event that just doesn't align with our overall brand, then a standard response might be, "Thank you for the invitation to speak at your event. Adam's schedule does not allow him to be at that event this year. And...I have a great recommendation for a speaker who I think would align well with your mission and vision for the event. Would it be all right if I made an introduction?" Say no and offer a solution. Always. This likely just saved you and your Executive hours of work on something that wasn't really right for him or for the organization.

When someone stops by your desk to just "ask you a quick question" or "chat for five minutes" and you're in the middle of a project or time block, you have to respect your time! This is truly about leading by example. Instead of dropping whatever you were working on, tell them you are in the middle of XYZ, and ask if you can schedule a fifteen-minute meeting with them later in the week so that you can give the conversation your full attention. If it can't wait, at least try to finish your project and get together with the person in an hour. It is likely not an emergency; it is simply the individual needing you to solve a problem for them. If you give it a little time, they will likely come up with a solution on their own. People are resourceful! And if they can't solve it on their own, well, then, you have set aside time when you can be focused and present to help them figure it out.

Lead by example. The more you value and respect your time, the more other people will too. Eventually, people will understand that emailing you to get on your calendar is the best use of everyone's time. Or they will just stop bothering you with random requests. Either way is a win for everyone's productivity!

Founders and Force Multipliers have to contend with a variety of distractions each day. Having strong emotional fitness and a solid energy management routine will go a long way toward helping you both handle whatever comes your way. Read on as Adam explains.

ACHIEVE MORE TOGETHER

- Do you respect your own time?
- Do you respect your leader/Force Multiplier's time?
- What are you currently saying yes to that doesn't align with your goals?
- Force Multipliers, is there a pattern of distractions and interruptions for you or your Executive? How can you mitigate those? Create a plan and implement.

MANAGE YOUR ENERGY

Part of a good personal growth practice is learning how to effectively and consistently manage your energy. Have you ever been in a meeting or at a family gathering, and you can just feel your eyes glaze over and you start thinking about your last marathon or the latest episode of *Survivor*? You're smiling and nodding at all the right spots. Your body is there, but you are *definitely* not. Why is that? The meeting you're in is probably one you requested. You love your family. You're a great listener and a brilliant conversationalist. So why can't you seem to stay there, in the moment?

Several things can be happening here, and they all come down to mindset, focus, and saying no. Let's work on this through the process of elimination.

Are you in a meeting, hanging out with friends, or conducting an interview, but your mind isn't there? Well, why did you say yes in the first place? Out of obligation? Fear of missing out? Because you're letting someone else or something else dictate your time and priorities? Because no one else can do it as well as you can? *Just stop!* The first step is saying no and making sure you're only doing the things and spending time with the people who are going to get you one step closer to your goals.

In *Outwitting the Devil,* by Napoleon Hill, the Devil makes a solid point: business leaders must be careful who they surround themselves with because negative mindset, low-level conversations, and mediocrity may cause drifting. Now, the Devil was referring to the aimless drifting of an individual, one who never finds or accomplishes their definite purpose in life, but either way—surround yourself with just anybody, and you will drift! Time is not a renewable resource. You've got industries to disrupt and lives to change. Ain't nobody got time for mediocrity.

Okay, so let's say you and your Executive Assistant have got this part down—you're surrounding yourself with the best people on the planet, and you're only saying yes to the critical meetings, activities, etc., that will move you and your business forward. Why are you still not present? It's time to do a mental and physical energy check. Have you exercised that day? Did you eat breakfast? Is it time for a snack? Maybe you simply need to get up, move, and grab some water, and then you'll be able to refocus immediately. Keep these things in mind. This is why I prime my body every day with exercise and proper nutrition. If I know I have X number of meetings that day (that I consciously said yes to), then I still need to make sure I'm 100 percent present in all of them, no matter if it's 8:00 a.m. or 4:00 p.m.

Taking that a step further, how's your mental and emotional fitness? Are you meditating, journaling regularly, and taking time to think and just breathe? These should be regular parts of your routine so that the possibility of drifting away during a board meeting and missing a crucial piece of information is mitigated. But stuff happens, and it's all about how you deal with it. If you are truly not in the right frame of mind or are mentally exhausted from a massive challenge the day before, then reschedule that interview. It would be a waste of time for both of you if, no matter how great they are, you don't like the candidate simply because you're not all there. It's okay to cancel that finance meeting if you know you just don't have it in you to make one more decision. It's just a different way of saying no.

Say no to the meeting so you can say yes to taking care of yourself so you are back at it full force the next day. Now, this shouldn't happen often if you're working on your mental, emotional, and physical fitness every day, but if it does happen, you just need to be prepared. I use a personal mantra to bring me back when I find myself drifting: "Right here, right now, in this moment." It grounds me and helps me refocus.

ACHIEVE MORE TOGETHER

- When do you find yourself "drifting" most often? Notice any patterns. Are those meetings or activities out of alignment with your natural behavior and/or goals? Are those activities something that you can eliminate or delegate to your Executive Assistant?
- Create a proactive energy management routine.
- Force Multipliers, get your Executive's buy-in to hold them accountable to managing their energy. Better yet, hold each other accountable!
- Where do you need to practice more presence in your life?

DECISION FATIGUE

For an Executive, managing your energy allows you to make better decisions on a daily, weekly, and annual basis, as well as helps you mitigate decision fatigue. Decision fatigue is not just another pop psychology buzz phrase. Decision fatigue is the deteriorating quality of decisions made by an individual after a long session of decision-making. And what do Executives do all day? They make decisions. Executive Assistants can have a major impact on their Executive's decision-making capabilities, thus impacting the entire organization.

DECISION FATIGUE IS REAL

At some point, you will just have too many decisions to make and too many people coming at you from every angle asking for your time, your money, your advice, your ideas, etc. Anticipate it, plan for it, and do everything in your power to maintain your energy levels in order to be completely there, wherever you are, whoever you are with.

HOW TO MITIGATE EXECUTIVE DECISION FATIGUE

The first step is to mitigate the number of decisions you make throughout the day. If you've noticed, top Executives often have a work uniform that allows them to make one less decision each day. Mine is a pair of Allbirds, jeans, a T-shirt with an inspirational message designed by my company, and a hoodie on chilly days.

What other decisions can you eliminate? Workouts? Meals? Can you organize your life (or work with your assistant to do it for you) in such a way that your daily choices become daily habits and you just don't have to think about the day-to-day minutiae? I think so. Delegate decision-making to your EA as much as possible to help streamline the decision-making process. For example, provide your meal preferences, and allow your EA to place the final order. The same goes for travel, meeting, or gift preferences.

Once the smaller, low-impact decisions are handled, it's time to move on to more critical decisions. By understanding the best time and most effective way to prepare an issue for their Executive, Force Multipliers facilitate the final decision. For example, your EA can handle all the detailed questions and help the Director of Marketing formulate a strong proposal before bringing it to their Executive. Or your EA can do all of the planning for a board meeting and bring two agenda options to you—all you need to do is choose the one you want to move ahead with.

THE 40/70 RULE FOR EXECUTIVES AND EXECUTIVE ASSISTANTS

For Executive Assistants, it's also important to balance the need to be over-prepared and to plan everything out down to the very last detail, with a sense of urgency to keep moving the business forward. Sometimes, it's better to act than it is to wait on one more piece of information.

Take the 40/70 Rule, for example. Former Secretary of State Colin Powell created the 40/70 Rule that explains this concept. This rule states that leaders should make decisions when they have between 40 and 70 percent of the information needed. If you make a decision with less than 40 percent of the information, you're shooting from the hip. But if you wait until you have more than 70 percent of the information, you could get stuck or overwhelmed, and you may risk the productivity and effectiveness of your entire organization.

Force Multipliers must keep the 40/70 Rule in mind when working with their leader. If you wait too long to present a problem or issue to your Executive for a decision, you might lose customers because they get impatient and go to a competitor who can fulfill their needs faster. You might have employees who do unnecessary damage because they are waiting for your Executive to make a decision. Or your company could lose revenue because you aren't willing to take a risk without having all the information.

You'll have to analyze your percentage and weigh where you are at. If you're at 20 percent, you have to get more information. If you're at 80 percent, then you may have waited too long. If you are between 40 and 70 percent then you and your Executive will have to rely on your intuition, prior experience, and best judgment. That is where the most effective leaders are born. Executive Assistants can get the team and information to between 40 and 70 percent and then turn it over to the Executive to pull the trigger.

WHY ONE MORE DECISION IS ONE TOO MANY

Executives make decisions all day, so sometimes having to make just one more decision is one too many. That one more usually comes from their EA or Chief of Staff. As frustrating as it is when your Executive won't give you an answer to something you think is cut and dry and one of the easiest decisions they will make that day (like if they want a massage or not), it's not that simple. Decision fatigue makes small, seemingly inconsequential decisions easier to push off. As the Executive Assistant, your job is to remember the question and ask it again at a better time. Your Executive probably knows this. They may be okay pushing off a decision with you (more than anyone else) because they trust you to remember and come back for a decision at a later date. That isn't always true with everyone else in your organization.

HOW EXECUTIVE ASSISTANTS CAN MOVE FORWARD WITHOUT A DECISION

So what can Executive Assistants do when they're waiting on a decision? Plan ahead as much as you can. What are your Executive's decision fatigue triggers? Are there things that they always leave until the last minute to decide on? Gifts? Travel plans? Dinner reservations? Meeting agendas? Speeches? As long as there is no money on the line, book or plan these ahead of time. Book dinner at three of your Executive's favorite restaurants for business meetings, and then cancel the other two once they are ready to make the decision. Schedule that massage for when your Executive lands in Austin—just make sure you put a reminder in your calendar to cancel the massage twenty-four hours in advance if necessary.

Pay attention to what is getting pushed off. If you have access to your Executive's email and you or other people are emailing him questions but they are just getting deleted, make a note of those questions. If they are not pressing, go over them in person in your weekly one-to-one meeting. This goes for meetings they aren't ready to commit to or issues they aren't ready to deal with. Make a note. Get as much information as possible, and then bring it back to their attention in a few days or weeks later, depending on how time-sensitive the issue is. By identifying their decision procrastination triggers, you can set proactive deadlines and time block for the time crunch. For example, if you know that before every speech, your Executive likes to make last-minute changes, just make sure the night before a big presentation, you plan for a late night at the office.

NAVIGATING COMPETING PRIORITIES

No matter how much you are on the same page, your priorities for the day may just not be your Executive's priorities. You're just trying to get your work done as efficiently as possible: getting a meeting rescheduled, making sure there is an agenda for next week's meeting, finalizing travel, and doing all the things that your Executive asked you to take care of. But they may be dealing with an employee crisis that you aren't even aware of yet, or perhaps your Executive is stalling because it's necessary to get a pulse on the organization before making a final decision. Remember, stay open and curious. There may be more going on behind the scenes.

Sometimes, Executives just can't make one more decision. EAs must understand the Executive's perspective. With people coming at us all day, we feel like our options and our freedom are being taken away. So when our EA pops in asking us what time we want to leave for New York or if we want to attend a charity function in three weeks, we push off the decision (which, yes, I know means you can't get your work done). We're just not ready to commit to anything else that will take up our time. Try us again later.

FOCUS ON WHAT YOU CAN DECIDE

Focus on what you can decide for your Executive. Work within agreed-upon parameters, and take those decisions off their plate before decision fatigue leads to decision avoidance and no one gets anything done! Help your Executive by giving them options. Instead of asking an open-ended question like "Where do you want to take the leadership team on a retreat this year?" come with three solid options of where, when, and the activities available and why the group would enjoy each. Then all your Executive has to say is yes or no, and add in skydiving. Simple. Easy. Done.

Remember, your Executive should not be part of planning meetings (that includes with you). They need to make decisions, not plans. By facilitating that process, you are solidifying your role as a strategic business partner.

While decision fatigue can happen to the best of us, there are ways to combat it by making decisions ahead of time, delegating or delaying decision-making, and creating routines that help us stay centered and clear. And of course, making sure you schedule plenty of time for rest and recovery doesn't hurt.

ACHIEVE MORE TOGETHER

- What decisions can you eliminate, automate, or make once and be done?
- Force Multipliers, what projects or decisions does your Executive tend to push off? Take those off their plate.

RECOVERY TIME

When I was training for triathlons a few years ago, I thought a lot about what it means to be an athlete. Athletes don't just exercise; they train. They don't just eat; they fuel. They don't just race; they compete. They don't just rest; they recover. These are all critical strategies for being a world-class athlete. So how can we apply these same concepts to the business world and create corporate athletes?

I know that most of you already think like athletes in terms of growth (if you didn't, you wouldn't be reading this book). You want to improve day after day and are always working on that next goal. But what really sets athletes apart is not the training, the competition, the fueling—it's the recovery. We have to start thinking like athletes who put extreme focus on recovery—emotional, physical, mental, social, professional, and spiritual recovery.

PRIORITIZE RECOVERY LIKE AN ATHLETE

Remember, all gains are made in recovery. Have you ever seen cyclists after a big competition? They will literally lie down, legs out straight, and not move after a race. When you break down muscle fibers during intense exercise, they rebuild themselves stronger during your recovery periods in order to be prepared for the next intense session.

The same can be applied to your business. Entrepreneurs, leaders, business owners, and Executive Assistants all work extremely hard, but too few of them make time for recovery. Without recovery, you'll break. Now, this doesn't mean you have to take weeks off at a time and completely unplug. In fact, too much recovery is bad for you. Think about it—sleeping fifteen hours a day will hurt your body and your emotional fitness. But on the flip side, too little sleep, like three to four hours a night, isn't beneficial to you either. You need to find the sweet spot. The optimal amount of recovery time will vary slightly from person to person, but we must make time for recovery of our minds, our souls, and our bodies. This recovery time will, in turn, make us stronger and better leaders and prepare us for the day ahead.

After an intense day at the office, we must allow time for the cells in our minds to recover and rebuild in order to handle the next big stimulus (i.e., problem). Think of it as a staircase. You step up (intense session that breaks down your mind/body), and then there is a flat landing (recovery session). This repeats over and over again on your way up the stairs (growth). As you recover, each step becomes easier, and your growth starts to compound.

So the key is to incorporate recovery points throughout your day. Here are a few examples:

- Sleep seven to nine hours each night (which means you'll have to say no to things at night in order to go to bed early. Nothing good happens after 8:30 p.m. anyway!).

- Take five minutes every ninety minutes to clear your mind, breathe, meditate, or do some push-ups or handstands—whatever will clear your mind in order for you to recover and refocus.
- In the middle of the day, take twenty to thirty minutes to breathe, read a book, meditate, or go for a walk.
- Set aside an hour in the morning to start your day with meditation, journaling, reading, or just sitting and being with yourself.
- Add thirty to forty-five minutes of daily exercise—just get moving! Run, walk, dance, swim, do yoga or martial arts, hike, chop wood. Just do something that creates energy within your body. This is where clarity comes from.

Start small. You don't need to master recovery in one day. Start by taking a ten-minute break and walking around your office, or turn your chair away from your computer screen and practice deep breathing. Just stop and be. You will start to feel the effects of these recovery periods almost immediately. Once you start with these small recovery points, you'll eventually start adding more recovery time to your life, which leads to increased productivity. Yes, it seems counterintuitive, but sometimes you really do need to slow down to speed up.

MANAGE YOUR TEAM MEMBERS' RECOVERY

As a leader, you'll have to take this one step further. My Ironman training coach always liked to remind me that his number-one job when coaching professional athletes is to manage their recovery. It's his job to know when to make them stop. Just like my coach manages his athletes, you must actively manage the recovery of your team members, and perhaps no one needs that help more than your EA. Create daily recovery periods for everyone. Push your team hard, push for the results, but allow for recovery time. Take a group walk, do ten jumping jacks on the hour every hour, have a dance party at three o'clock in the afternoon.

More importantly, encourage them to take vacations and long weekends or leave early when they need to. And don't forget to role-model the behavior you wish to see. I have known Executives who won't even put up "out of office" messages on their email because they are afraid others will judge them for taking time off. What sort of message do you think that sends to their employees? Don't do that. Instead, lead the way and proudly post that out of office message!

Build these recovery habits for yourself and your team, and you'll be building a big life and big business faster and more effectively. Recovery equals results.

WEEKEND WARRIOR

Good time management and recovery time doesn't just happen Monday through Friday. These principles of discipline, energy management, and prioritization apply to the weekends as well. Use your weekends wisely, especially if you are one of those people who has a bad case of the Mondays—every Monday. You know? The Sunday Scaries? Do you sing song lyrics like "It's just another manic Monday" or "But whenever Monday comes you can find me cryin' all of the time" on your commute into the office each week? Well, you're definitely not alone. I think you have two choices here:

1. Refresh your resume and start looking for another job. Clearly you are not happy or fulfilled in your current position if you are dreading Mondays.

2. Refresh your weekends so that you are setting yourself up for a successful week. If you genuinely enjoy your work and career, you may just need a reboot.

While the seven-day week can be traced back four thousand years to Babylon, the first recorded mention of a weekend wasn't until 1879. Back then, the weekend was a half day on Saturday and a full day on Sunday. In 1908, a New England mill was the first American factory to institute the five-day workweek we know today: a full day of rest on Saturday and Sunday. So how can you maximize that time in order to have a productive week?

Here are five things I recommend Executives, Entrepreneurs, and yes, Executive Assistants too, do every weekend in order to rest, recover, and prepare themselves for a week of minimal stress and maximum results:

1. HAVE A FAMILY MEETING

Whether your family includes yourself, your in-laws, and your five children, or it's just you and your partner, schedule a weekly family meeting for thirty minutes to an hour. This is the perfect time to connect to discuss the week ahead—who's picking up the kids, what late-night meetings you might have, dinner plans with friends, or special events. Syncing up your calendars is a must. It's also a good time to talk about any upcoming household items that need to be taken care of (like finding a new landscaping company or scheduling a handyman for repairs). Don't forget to get on the same page with finances. Are there any big purchases coming up? Perhaps you want to aggressively pay down some debt. Discuss, and make a plan. Then check in weekly during your family meeting so that you actually make progress on these goals. Involve the kids as soon as they are old enough. Start them young learning about financial management and time management, and they will be ahead of 95 percent of the adult population. Have fun! Grab your favorite coffee and get down to business. If you schedule these conversations weekly, you will significantly cut down on the mundane, uninspiring conversations with your partner and family throughout the week and have much more time for deeper and more meaningful interactions. Bringing your Executive Assistant into these meetings is optional. She could participate and make any on-the-fly changes to the schedule, or you can keep it in the family and simply relay the changes to your EA after the fact.

HALLIE NARRATES

My family consists of myself, my husband (Bill), and our two mutts (Enzo and Stella). We all show up at the dining room table at 10:00 a.m. on Sundays. Bill makes the coffee. I bring the calendar. Bill has an unpredictable schedule, including several meetings and trainings throughout the week outside of his regular hours. I often travel several times throughout the month. We both work a lot and could end up being two ships passing in the night if we didn't make it a priority to get on the same page. Every Sunday, we meet to go over our schedules in depth to make sure we each have errands covered, know who is on doggy duty, and in general just know where the other is during the week! We also plan at least one date night. At this meeting, we also go over our financials. We have specific investment goals, so we make sure we are on track and transfer funds into the appropriate accounts, as well as discuss any big trips or expenses that are coming up (hello, taxes!). This has been such an important part of our marriage; I highly recommend you institute weekly family meetings.

2. SCHEDULE WORKOUTS

Exercise has such a huge impact on all areas of your life—mental clarity, focus, energy, health, and nutrition choices. Exercise truly leaks into all areas of your life. Use working out as a conduit to being a better leader, partner, and friend. Take the time to plan your workouts on the weekends. Yes, your EA probably already scheduled workout blocks in your calendar, but don't forget to actually plan out what you are going to be doing during the allotted times so that you're not just aimlessly taking selfies in the gym mirror. Have a plan, and then execute. Better yet, get a trainer or coach who will tell you exactly what to do during your workout time.

HALLIE NARRATES

Working out consistently is something that I have struggled with for years. I have added scheduling workouts into my weekend planning session in order to change this. Every week, as I'm going over my schedule with Bill, I also make sure I am scheduling all of my workouts. Depending on my work schedule, after-hours events, and date nights, more often than not that means I have to work out in the morning. Not my preferred time to work out, but I've got goals.

3. MEAL PLAN AND PREP

Exercise and nutrition go hand in hand. To be the best version of you, you have to take care of yourself first. That starts on the weekend. Yes, it can be time-consuming, but the investment of time on the weekends—planning out your meals, prepping protein, cutting up veggies, and portioning out snacks—will save you a ton of time during the week. It will also help you reach your health goals. You can save even more time by using a meal-prep service or getting your groceries delivered. As the great Ben Franklin said, "If you fail to plan, you are planning to fail!"

HALLIE NARRATES

This is a critical one for me as well. I am on a fitness and health journey to transform my lifestyle indefinitely, so making sure I have healthy meals and snacks prepared for the week is essential. I usually portion out snacks such as macadamia nuts and veggies. I also prep and portion out all of my lunches (for example, salmon and roasted vegetables or chicken and acorn squash). I also make two meals on the weekend that can last the week. Even if I don't prep everything ahead, I have meals and snacks planned for each day so I never have to think about what I'm eating or when. In a pinch, soup, protein shakes, or eggs are great go-tos!

4. SET WEEKLY GOALS

Regardless of what system you use (Best Self Journal, a basic planner, Todist, Weekly Execution Plan, etc.), make sure you are strategically looking at what you need to accomplish during the week ahead to get you closer to your monthly and annual goals. What you do this week will move you either forward or backward. Make every day count. Focus on the revenue-generating activities that will move you and your business forward. Identify the three to five big things you need to accomplish, and then make sure you block time into your calendar during the week to work on them. Remember, if it is not scheduled, it's not real. Once it's in your calendar, as long as you honor your commitment to yourself and do the "important thing" when it's scheduled in your calendar, your results will be inevitable. Again, this is a great time to loop your EA into the conversation and make sure you are on the same page for the week ahead.

5. UNPLUG

One of the most important things you can do is unplug! Take time to rest and recover, whatever that looks like for you—hiking, skiing with the family, spa time, or reading a good book at home. You can't be effective and productive if you are "on" all the time. Now, just like unplugging looks different for different people, the amount of time needed to unplug varies too. Some people need an entire forty-eight hours with no work emails, while others just need a couple of nonwork hours each day. Do what works for you, but honor that time. If you're unplugged, be unplugged and present in whatever moment you are in. Recharge and get ready for a kick-ass week ahead!

for a hike with your partner, take your kids to the movies, get a massage, sleep in! Whatever your go-to is to decompress and rejuvenate, do that.

I've been following the above routine for years. For me, the weekend is a great mix of time with the family, time to read and think about my business, time outdoors with my kids, time for great conversations with my wife, and time getting organized and ready to crush the week ahead. If you do this every weekend, you will have a competitive advantage over the majority of the population. Having the discipline to have a purposeful and productive weekend sets you up for massive success. Not everyone is willing to do these things. But discipline equals freedom. And isn't that what we're all after?

BONUS: THE SUNDAY NIGHT SHIFT

If you want to take your job as a weekend warrior a step further, here are three additional tactics I use on Sunday nights to make the shift from weekends to the workweek:

1. Do a detailed review of your calendar based on your current company objectives and shifting priorities. Add or cancel meetings as necessary. For example, you may need to postpone an interview for a new controller if you have a development deal that needs to be renegotiated at the eleventh hour. This is when you start firing off a string of emails to your Executive Assistant.

2. Email your leadership team or your direct reports with any ideas you had over the weekend that you would like them to explore or take action on, any questions, and any new directives for the week. The weekends offer great time to reflect and gain clarity, so you may be shifting course the following

week. Make sure you communicate that to your team and, most importantly, to your EA!

3. Check your energy and alignment. This is all about mentally and emotionally preparing to bring your best self into the office on Monday. Is there anything bothering you that you need to work through? Do it. Maybe that means doing an extra meditation session or an intense workout, journaling, or calling a trusted mentor. Make sure you are ready to show up and do work on Monday.

HALLIE NARRATES

I couldn't agree more. During the week, from the moment Executive Assistants wake up until the moment their heads hit their pillows, they are on. I don't mean they just show up to the office and sip coffee while scrolling through Instagram and occasionally answering the phone. I mean they are responding to emails while they eat breakfast, scheduling social media posts as they slip on their stilettos, listening to leadership books while they grab a latte, and preparing for meetings between meetings. They don't just show up; they step up and step into any role that needs to be filled that day, or any other day, for their Executive.

It can easily get overwhelming if you don't have measures in place to streamline your days and weeks. Like many Executive Assistants and Chiefs of Staff, my weeks are packed, so I use the weekend to set myself up for a successful week ahead. Every Sunday I spend several hours planning and preparing for the upcoming week. Yup, just like Adam does. He has taught me well!

In addition to Adam's five tips for using the weekend to set you up for the week ahead, I have a few more just for the Executive Assistants. I hope these will help you enter the week feeling a little less stressed, more in control of your time and schedule, and even more badass than I know you already are.

1. **Call family.** While you're meal prepping and cooking is the perfect time to call your parents, siblings, in-laws, best friends, etc., and catch up. Everyone's in a good mood on a Sunday morning after a fresh cup of coffee.

2. **Review your Executive's schedule.** I used to review Adam's calendar every Friday afternoon to confirm any meetings and make sure there weren't any outstanding items I needed to prepare for his meetings or training events for the week. While our Executive Assistant now handles all of that, I do review Adam's schedule every Sunday and make recommendations on any adjustments needed, or I check in with our EA on upcoming events that we both need on our radar. Then, when our EA and I have our Monday meeting, we review Adam's schedule together, along with any action items we need to tackle.

3. **Prepare and anticipate questions.** Every Monday morning I meet with Adam for thirty minutes. In order to maximize our meeting, I prepare any questions or important items on Sunday night after reviewing Adam's calendar. We may go over presentations for the week, look at the travel schedule, or move through a list of items I need a decision on. In addition to preparing questions for him, I make sure to anticipate his questions in order to have that information ready (such as number of potential attendees at an event, contract negotiation points, or options for reorganizing a division) so we can both move forward with our priorities for the week.

4. **Plan outfits.** I am a huge proponent of the office uniform and basically only wear jeans, a blouse, and a blazer in either black, white, navy, or beige. Why overcomplicate it? I do like to fancy it up with some gold or turquoise jewelry and leopard-print heels every now and then. I also look at my calendar and plan accordingly. If I have

a presentation or important interview, I may go more business formal than if I have a solo day in the office following up on emails or writing content. Regardless, it's still black, white, navy, or beige. Perhaps you have a little more fun with your fashion than I do, which means it's even more important to plan your outfits—including jewelry and shoes. It makes one less thing to worry about during your whirlwind week.

5. **Plan and schedule social media posts.** If you manage social media for your Executive or have an avid following of your own, then plan your content and schedule your posts ahead of time. In the past, I've used Hootsuite and Buffer to schedule posts such as inspirational quotes, thought-provoking questions, articles or blogs of interest, career opportunities, upcoming training events, and personal photos or anecdotes. It's not always perfect, and there are things that often come up in real time that are more relevant. But this way, you always have content planned and ready to go to continue to build the brand, provide value, and increase engagement, whether that is for you or for your Executive. Real-time events that come up are just bonuses.

Creating time in your calendar every day for a bit of recovery will keep you fresh and thriving. And using your weekends wisely is a great way to set yourself up for success each week. Need some ideas for what to do during your recovery time? Let's dive into some self-care strategies with Adam.

ACHIEVE MORE TOGETHER

- Are you role-modeling recovery time for your team?
- What are some easy recovery points you can add into your day?
- For the next month, try out some of the weekend suggestions to set yourself up for a successful week. Challenge each other to implement these best practices, compare notes, and make adjustments that will optimize your weeks.
- Force Multipliers, try out the Weekly Execution Plan for annual goal setting and weekly prioritization.

SELF-CARE FOR SUCCESS

While both Executive Assistants and Executives can benefit from this chapter about self-care, this one is really for the EAs. That said, I would encourage Executives to read on. The more you can understand each other's perspectives and appreciate the challenges of your unique roles, the closer you will get to that symbiotic partnership.

One of the complaints we hear most often from Executive Assistants is that they don't have much time for themselves. They are often subject to the whims of others, but what about their own needs and desires? EAs might be on call, working nights and weekends, traveling with their Executive, etc. Executive Assistants are constantly dealing with competing priorities and demands. EAs are often not in control of their time, their tasks, or their day. They are heavily relied upon by their Executive (and often hundreds of people in an organization), and that's a lot of responsibility to shoulder. EAs are privy to confidential, sometimes highly charged information, a burden that may cause forced or self-imposed isolation.

Yes, all of this is by choice. EAs don't deny that. And yes, there can be a lot of perks and intrinsic value to being in the EA position. But the fact of the matter is that EAs, perhaps more than anyone else, need to make sure they are setting aside time to rest, recharge, and recover. Most Executives make this a priority; why shouldn't EAs?

WHAT IS SELF-CARE?

Self-care is the right and responsibility to take care of your physical, emotional, and spiritual well-being. Self-care is about knowing which needs you want to fulfill and knowing how you want to feel and seeking out nourishing and nurturing activities that will meet those needs and generate those feelings. Self-care is doing whatever you need to do (healthfully) to take care of your mind, body, and soul with activities that *you* control. Self-care is about thriving, not just coping.

Operating from this place enhances your ability to make not only more decisions, but better decisions. While you can certainly whip out a quick breathing technique or do some push-ups on the fly, you will get the most benefits by consistently practicing a self-care routine. Self-care is healthcare.

Self-care routines can look a little different for everyone, but they generally include some of the following: exercise, journaling, breathing, yoga, prayer, sitting in silence, or meditation. Why these activities? Because they are all designed to go inward, to allow thoughts to come and go with no attachment to the outcome. They create a space for you to just *be*. And if you're anything like me, these are the times when you get the most clarity and the best ideas: when you are simply in the moment, just being. No agenda. No expectations. When this becomes a part of your daily life, just think how much more effective you will be when you're hit with the hard stuff of running a business and the tough leadership decisions.

Self-care can be a part of your daily life, and you don't always need to invest a lot of time to feel the effects. You can enhance your self-care by including more occasional activities such as vacations, massages, yoga or meditation retreats, spa days, shopping sprees, or mission trips. If indulged in regularly, these simply wouldn't have the same effect (and might hurt your wallet, which could cause more stress!). Focusing on a daily self-care practice will have the biggest impact long term. This is the daily recovery that will allow you to keep up with and stay ahead of your Executive.

Examples of ways you can incorporate self-care and recovery into your daily routine include:

- Setting concrete boundaries around your time (for your Executive and your friends and family)
- Committing to a daily exercise routine
- Practicing meditation and relaxation techniques
- Starting a gratitude journal
- Creating a prayer routine
- Spending quality time with friends and family
- Taking a walk in nature
- Getting creative with writing or art
- Getting enough sleep
- Fueling your body with healthy food
- Finding a constructive outlet for overwhelming emotions and allowing them the time and space they need
- Taking a bath
- Reading by candlelight

Right before we hired an EA in late 2017, Hallie realized just how critical it was to have a self-care routine. She hadn't been purposeful about self-care before and would indulge in a self-care activity (though really it was a coping mechanism) only when she was on the brink of burnout. Her daily self-care routine now includes exercise, lots of water, nutritious food, plenty of sleep, and reading a fiction book every night before bed.

Whatever method of self-care you choose, ensure that it is simple, easy to do, and consistent. Don't overcomplicate it. You have enough things to worry about. Making sure your self-care practice is perfect shouldn't be one of them. But do choose something. If you want to be able to keep up with your Executive, let alone stay one step ahead, you've got to be taking care of your mind, body, and energy.

ACHIEVE MORE TOGETHER

- When do you feel your most centered, peaceful, and aligned? How can you create those experiences and moments throughout your day?
- Create a self-care routine. Don't overcomplicate it.

PART FIVE

ACHIEVE MORE TOGETHER

HOW TO FIND YOUR MATCH

Now that you know what the ideal partnership looks like, it's time to start searching. Or perhaps you're already in a partnership that is less than ideal, and you're looking to replace your current Executive Assistant with a high performer. How the hell do you find one of these unicorns?

First, we already know that you need a Force Multiplier—no question. For Entrepreneurs or leaders of multiple businesses, you need a jack-of-all-trades with strong leadership and business acumen who can take your ideas and make them happen while organizing all the details of your life and business along the way. You need someone who will extend your reach further on social media, in the community, and in your company. A great Executive Assistant will allow you to do your job faster and more effectively. You need an EA who will handle the details so you can stay in your strength zone, working on the strategy (better yet, she will help with strategy, too, so you can really focus on the future). Sometimes it takes a leader years (and a rotating door of EAs) to find the right fit, just like it can take an Executive Assistant a while to find an Executive who challenges her and helps her grow.

Let's increase the hiring success rate so you can both get down to business.

KNOW WHO YOU ARE LOOKING FOR

This would be a great time to revisit Chapter 4 ("What's in a Name?"). The first step in finding the right Executive Assistant is being very clear on who you are looking to partner with in your life and business. Depending on where you are in your career or business, you may be looking for a Personal Assistant, a Chief of Staff, or an Operations Coordinator. Get clear before you spend time recruiting and interviewing. No sense in wasting your time or theirs.

ATTRACT TALENT

You're looking for top talent, right? High performers and high achievers want to be surrounded by other high performers and high achievers. Executive Assistants who are at the top of their game are leaders in their own right. They are going to need a very strong leader and someone with a compelling vision in order to continue on their career trajectory. If a top-level EA doesn't align with a leader with a strong vision who's driven to succeed, it's just not going to be the right fit.

Are you top talent? Who do you have to be in order to attract talent at the level you want? Here's a simple litmus test for you: what questions do people ask you most often? Are people asking you for a new fitness program, business best practices, career advice, real estate negotiation tips, best new restaurants or bars, book recommendations, exciting new Netflix shows to binge-watch, or the secrets to a successful marriage? Those questions that people ask you are what you're known for—whether you like it or not. I know there is more to you than your Netflix addiction, but if that is what people are asking you about, then right or wrong, that's the brand you've developed. As an Entrepreneur, you are the brand, so be conscious and careful about what you're putting out into the universe. Perception is reality. If you don't like the questions people are asking, it's time to make a change!

What are you doing every day to cause others to want to be led by you? How are you increasing your leadership lid daily? If you don't have a personal and professional development plan in place, create one (books, journaling, fitness routine, meditation, conferences, etc.). The level of talent you attract is going to be a direct reflection of what kind of leader you are. You must lead yourself first before anyone else will follow. This is particularly true for Executive Assistants. Because an EA's success is so closely tied to the success of an Executive, the Executive must be consistently communicating their vision, mission, and values in order to catch the attention of a talented Executive Assistant.

ALWAYS BE RECRUITING

If you're not already, start paying attention to your brand. Your brand includes everything from what you wear for speaking engagements to your social media presence, your logo, your website, the language you use in your blog, your job ads, and the charities that you choose to donate to. Yes, it all matters. Building your brand takes time, but it is one of the best ways to attract talent. With a clear message and brand, prospective candidates don't have to guess about whether or not your company would be the right fit; it's all just out there. Again, this is doubly important when we're talking about looking for your right hand. You want them to know what they are getting into. Better yet, you only want applicants who are down with your idiosyncrasies.

I know you're already sharing your vision with everyone you meet. Do it even more. Ask all of your contacts (and strangers) whether they know anyone who's up to the challenge of joining you on your entrepreneurial journey. Share exactly who you are looking for. Share your company's culture. Share your organization's successes and failures. Tell the story, tell the story, tell the story. The right people will start showing up.

FIND THE RIGHT BEHAVIORAL MATCH

I think an important part of hiring is ensuring you have the right behavioral match for the position. Have your candidates complete a behavior assessment. Remember, there are always variables with online testing and self-reporting. The best practice is to verify the behavior assessment with your candidate and use it as a tool to get to know them better. Only weigh the assessment as 25 percent of the overall interview process. Other factors, like their track record of success, experience, and drive, will also come into play. But understanding behavior is a good baseline.

For example, if you are an Entrepreneur in your first eighteen months of operations and things are chaotic and changing every fifteen seconds, hiring an EA who naturally thrives in a calm and stable environment may not be a good fit. That EA may be a great fit for you when you're five years into the business. But right now you need someone who can run with you and pick up the pieces without missing a beat (or having a nervous breakdown). It's all about alignment. You never have the wrong person. Just the wrong job for the person at the time.

WHAT TO LOOK FOR WHEN HIRING A FORCE MULTIPLIER

Once you have lined up several interviews with candidates and have determined that they are good behavioral matches, there are a few additional things to look for:

- **The ideal Force Multiplier is professional.** I wish this went without saying, but unfortunately, that's not always the case. Your strategic partner must be discerning, competent, respectful, and gracious and must maintain strict confidentiality. They need to be calm amid the chaos. They are an extension of you and represent you at all times, so choose wisely. Pay particular attention to how candidates are speaking about former bosses and colleagues because this is how they will talk about you in the future, should you ever part ways.
- **They are a driver.** Someone who takes initiative and is the catalyst for growth and change is so important for a leader. An "order taker" will not work for high-achieving business leaders. You need someone who makes things happen, even if you haven't asked. I like to look for entrepreneurial endeavors as well. This can include volunteer work, helping friends create websites, blogging, coaching their kid's soccer team, or selling their paintings on Etsy. Are they a part of their church, a network marketing company, or a local Business Network International group? They are not content with a nine-to-five. They want more. This signals to me that they are driven, hungry, and not afraid to work for their goals.
- **They challenge your thinking.** I know you think you want a "yes-man" or "yes-woman," but trust me: you don't. You will have enough of those individuals in your life as you build a team and organization. What you need from your Force Multiplier is a truth-teller. Someone who will say the things that need to be said, even when you don't want to hear them.

This individual will bring new perspectives to the table and force you to consider them from all angles. They will challenge your thinking, piss you off more than once, and have a distinct viewpoint to add to the conversation, all in the effort to help you make better decisions for your life and for the company.

- **They are not afraid to try new things.** You're not going to stop pushing forward and testing out ideas, so you need a Force Multiplier who is not afraid to do the same. Yes, they will challenge your thinking if the decision seems reckless, but after you've disagreed and committed to a course of action (even if it pushes them outside of their comfort zone), they're going to do it. Growth is the name of the game. You need to hire someone who is willing and eager to play.

- **They are fast-paced, intense, responsive, and adaptable.** Most leaders are just as impatient as I am. Couple that with high standards, and you can bulldoze over some of the best people. You're fast-paced and intense. Plus, you're highly responsive to challenges, the needs of your team, and the changes in your organization and industry. You need a Force Multiplier who can run with you and navigate constantly changing priorities (and when you just change your mind), someone who has a high sense of urgency and can switch between tasks and projects quickly. That isn't to say they aren't also highly efficient, organized, and detail-oriented. Fast and accurate are not mutually exclusive.

- **They are a strategic thinker and a creative problem-solver.** Force Multipliers understand how to assess current needs, evaluate all options while taking into account historic data and future goals, and ask the right questions to get results. They can tackle a problem from multiple angles, find a solution, and then close the loop.

- **They are resourceful.** No problem is too big or task too small for a Force Multiplier. They will figure it out, make sure it's handled, and get the job done. Ask for specific examples of how they made the impossible possible. Have they been able to navigate a particularly complex challenge? Do they like solving problems, and are they not afraid to take on more? Are they able to just make things happen regardless of what obstacles might be in the way? That will be your first indication of just how resourceful a candidate is and how far they are willing to go (legally and ethically, of course!) to get the job done.

- **They have exceptional written and oral communication skills.** Your Force Multiplier will often be communicating on your behalf—through memos, emails, social media, meetings, and more. Pay close attention to how candidates communicate online, as well as how they communicate with you and other team members throughout the hiring process. Your Executive Assistant not only has to be able to communicate with you, but they also will need to be able to interpret what you are saying and echo and enhance that message throughout the organization and to the public by many different means of communication. Make sure they can synthesize your ideas and vision and communicate them to the organization in such a way that inspires action.

- **They are a generalist.** A powerful Force Multiplier is a jack-of-all-trades. They have a wide array of interests, know a little about a lot, and enjoy researching, reading, and collecting information on many different subjects. A thirst for knowledge and natural curiosity often leave Force Multipliers lacking expertise in one specific area, but this is actually an advantage. If anything, a Force Multiplier's "specialty" lies in putting the pieces of a puzzle together with only a partial picture on the box cover to guide them (that inevitably changes halfway through the project) while under a tight deadline. This requires the ability to connect the dots from seemingly disparate information sources. It also requires adaptability, flexibility, and resourcefulness to get things done—all key generalist traits. Dig into what your candidates are reading and learning. A great question to ask is "What are you curious about right now?" And, of course, pay close attention to the questions they are asking you.

- **They have zero ego.** A great Force Multiplier prefers to lead from behind. They are not interested in the accolades or the spotlight. Their success and career satisfaction is derived from making you look great. Humility is paramount in this influential leadership role.

- **They are not offended by the way you work.** I heard this quote from a mastermind recently, and I think it's a really important concept when hiring a Force Multiplier: "Hire people who want to work the way you work, who don't get offended by the way you work." This just about sums it up. Your Force Multiplier must remain objective and take the ego out of the equation as much as possible. If you like to work long hours or short, if you like to run hard and fast for twelve weeks and then take two weeks off, if you like to go over every decision in detail and then change your mind twenty-four hours later, if you like to talk about your weekend or if you don't, it doesn't matter. You simply need to align yourself with a Force Multiplier who gets it, gets you, and isn't offended by how you roll.

- **They are a leader.** EAs also have the unique challenge of having to lead without a title. They must lead up to their Executive, and they must lead out to their colleagues, to business partners, and to the general public, all without a formal title or perceived authority. They must be able to lead through influence.

- **They own their mistakes and failures.** When you ask about mistakes or failures, you're not looking for anything specific, but rather what someone might consider a big mistake. What a candidate believes to be a big mistake might be a minor blip in my day. Will she be able to handle the big mistakes that happen in your life and company? Are they even willing to admit that they made mistakes or failed? I'm sure they learned from it (they'd better have!), but can they own it? Do they blame others and revert to a victim mentality? Or can they be humble enough to admit that they're not perfect?

- **They have a growth mindset.** Does the candidate have daily success habits that contribute to their learning and growth? What books are they reading? Are they listening to podcasts? Have they attended any voluntary training lately? Are they working on college credits or a certification? Having a thirst for knowledge and a desire to grow is going to be critical for a successful EA/Entrepreneur match.

Quite the tall order, isn't it? Do these individuals actually exist? They do! *And* they are rare.

Every time someone tells me they need to hire a Force Multiplier, I tell them to get started right away! They may not be planning to make a hire for a year or more, but it can sometimes take that long (depending on how much time they are committing to the search). You will want to interview a lot of people to really understand if they meet the aforementioned characteristics. Have your candidates take behavior assessments, shadow you for a day or week, and complete mock assignments to gauge their skills. This is an important partnership, and you should both do your due diligence.

Hallie is going to share what Executive Assistants should look for when partnering with a leader.

HALLIE NARRATES: WHAT TO LOOK FOR IN A LEADER

Executive Assistants, it's just as important for you to find your match by interviewing prospective leaders (and companies) and carefully considering who you choose to align yourself with.

Executives often ask me what Executive Assistants are looking for in a leader. After all, if a leader doesn't possess several important characteristics, then they are never going to attract the level of strategic partner they want. Leaders want to know who they need to be in order to hire and retain a top EA. And Force Multipliers want to know what a great leader looks like so they can create a mutually beneficial relationship that lasts years (or decades!).

Here's what I believe Force Multipliers should look for in a leader:

- **The ideal leader offers growth opportunities.** If you're not growing, you're dying. Cliché? Perhaps. True? Absolutely. When you're looking to partner with a leader, find out how previous EAs have grown in their roles. What are they doing now? How did the role evolve and responsibilities change over time? Are there opportunities to take on interesting projects or join committees? What sort of continuing education and training is supported by the company and, perhaps more importantly, the Exec? How have they grown in their career over the years? That will be a telltale sign about whether they are invested in growth in general—theirs or any of their team members'.
- **They challenge your thinking.** One of the most impactful things I have experienced working with Adam over the past eleven years is that he is constantly challenging my thinking. This includes offering a different perspective, pushing me to consider a problem from another angle, asking me pointed questions to get to the root of an

issue, and questioning my limiting beliefs. I'm not talking about just playing devil's advocate for the sake of being a contrarian (though there is some value in that too!). What I am talking about is getting me to think differently about myself, the challenges in front of me, and the world in general. It doesn't mean we always agree. But it always keeps me on my toes and curious about the world, our industry, other people, our team members, etc. That is growth.

- **They teach you how to lead.** First, a leader must lead by example and role-model the behavior they wish their staff to embody. But beyond this, a leader who is intentional about teaching their Force Multiplier how to lead is invaluable. Having access to your leader is imperative to making this happen. Make sure you find out how an Executive plans to communicate with you and how often. Will your weekly meetings take priority (or even happen at all)? How much access will you have to their email, calls, Slack, and meetings? Listening to how your leader communicates and how they handle challenges is one of the best ways to learn. Are they not only sharing the decisions that they made but explaining why and how that decision came to be? Are you even able to ask those questions? You need to be able to in order to have a true strategic partnership.

- **They push you outside of your comfort zone.** Great leaders are going to push you to get outside of your comfort zone—often. You will likely love your leader and hate your leader for it at the same time. But nothing breeds loyalty like someone who has helped you become a better version of yourself. A leader should be that for their assistant. The list of ways Adam has pushed me outside of my comfort zone is endless. They range from really minor experiences, like going on my first real roller-coaster, to bigger events, like speaking in front of ten thousand people, shooting a video for a global virtual EA summit, and hosting my first webinar series. I much prefer to be behind the scenes, and Adam knows this. That is why he doesn't allow me to stay there. I've helped facilitate classes and had to jump in on calls that I didn't think I was ready for. But Adam knew I was and, above all, had faith that I would figure it out, even if I failed a little along the way. Were these things incredibly uncomfortable? Yup. I think I'm still sweating from some of them. Did I learn and grow from these experiences? Absolutely. More than anything, I learned that challenging your team and influencing their personal and professional growth is the mark of a true leader.

- **They demonstrate honesty, trust, and integrity.** These may be harder to spot when interviewing, and trust, of course, comes with time. But do your research and listen between the lines to the Executive, as well as to current and former employees. Many leaders will hand out their references to candidates, but if they don't, ask. Their willingness to give you the contact information of current and former employees is often an answer in and of itself.

- **They are constantly raising their leadership lid.** Leaders must continue to grow and lead themselves first. If they don't continue to increase their leadership capital and leadership lid, their Executive Assistant may outgrow them (or a talented EA may not partner with them in the first place). There are so many amazing EAs who want more, but their Executive or organization is just not growing fast enough or is not ready to take the business to the next level. Ultimately those assistants leave for different opportunities with Executives who have much bigger visions, who are taking action and implementing. If leaders want to keep that top talent, then they have to work on growing themselves every day. Find out what books they are reading and what classes they have recently taken. Find out what they are curious about right now and how they are investing in themselves. Then, make sure it aligns with where you want to go and grow in your life and career.

- **They provide autonomy and freedom.** Executive Assistants need the freedom and flexibility to manage their work. They also need the latitude to make decisions and act. Leaders who don't allow Force

Multipliers to do their thing probably shouldn't have hired them in the first place. Ask questions to get a feel for an Executive's leadership and decision-making style. What issues do they want to know about, and what can simply be handled by you or someone else? What tasks or projects do they like to handle themselves, and does that mean you will be free to handle everything else? Find out what challenges they have had in the past with EAs and what they did and didn't like. If you are their first EA hire, staying in curiosity and figuring out their triggers for micromanagement may help alleviate issues down the line. But at the end of the day, leaders have chosen to hire an Executive Assistant to do what they do best: handle the 80 percent of an Exec's day-to-day so they can stay in their 20 percent. You both need to stay in your lane and have the autonomy and freedom to just get shit done. The right leader will not only understand this but will get out of your way so you can achieve more together, faster.

- **They are a visionary.** Force Multipliers want to work with a visionary. Someone who has a plan and the passion to make a mark on the world. Someone who is driven, has a growth mindset, and is playing the infinite game. A visionary who can see the future crystal clear and understands the need for a tactical genius and strategic partner to help them get there.

I have found the above to be some of the most common characteristics Executive Assistants look for in an Executive. But like all relationships in life, every EA–Executive partnership looks a little different based on the needs of both individuals. It's also important to recognize that those needs may change over time. The question to ask yourself is this: is your leader the right fit or the wrong fit for you? Ideally, you should determine this before accepting a position, but that doesn't always happen. You could be assigned to an Executive or be supporting your Executive's replacement. Even more common, you and your Executive may grow (or not) or have some big life events that change the working dynamic.

If that's the case, then it's time to reassess whether you are working for the right leader.

In fact, both Executive and Executive Assistant should make sure they are working with the right strategic partner.

ACHIEVE MORE TOGETHER

- Leaders, are you clear on what you are looking for in a Force Multiplier? What are your top three non-negotiables in a strategic partner?
- Force Multipliers, are you clear on what you are looking for in a leader? What are your top three non-negotiables?

ARE YOU WORKING WITH THE RIGHT STRATEGIC PARTNER?

Executive Assistants, if you are feeling unfulfilled at work, struggling to get excited about supporting and working with your Executive, or dreading going to the office in the morning—no matter how much you love being an Executive Assistant and no matter how great your company is—your Executive may not be the right fit for you. We've seen amazing EAs struggle and eventually leave because they want more growth and opportunity while their Executive is content with the status quo. Conversely, we've seen great EAs falter because their Executive is a hard driver and is constantly changing priorities and the EA would be better served in a more methodical and structured environment. Neither is right or wrong, better or worse—it's just not the right fit for either party.

ANALYZE THE SITUATION

If any of the above scenarios sounds like you, it's time to take a good hard look at yourself and your Executive. First, get clear on your own personality, behavior, working style, and career goals.

We've talked about behavior profiles in earlier chapters; make that a priority for yourself and your Executive. Take a look at your Executive's behavior or personality profile, and compare your results with his. Where are the assessments in alignment? Where is there a mismatch?

Some Executive Assistants want a strong, direct, fast-paced Executive. Others thrive in a more structured and copacetic environment, while still others will prefer working for a creative, spontaneous Executive. Do you like to keep it strictly business, or do you want to attend weekly dinners with your Executive and his family? Do you like a controlled and organized environment, or do you thrive on bringing order to chaos? Do you like to take the lead on all projects or do you prefer to wait for detailed instructions before tackling a task?

If you don't truly understand who you are and what you want, you'll constantly be searching without a clear direction. Instead, if you get clear on what works for you and what doesn't, then you can start working on your personal development and aligning yourself with the right people and career to mitigate the stress.

Take all of that into consideration as you are evaluating who you are and whether your Executive is the right fit for you.

HALLIE NARRATES

I know I am working for the right leader because I am constantly growing. I am challenged daily, and I take steps (okay, sometimes I'm pushed) outside of my comfort zone so that I can grow. I get up every day excited to go to work and help Adam grow our companies. I have freedom and flexibility with my work, and I am supported personally and professionally. Most importantly, I know I am working with the right leader because I don't have a boss but a business partner.

The EA-Executive relationship is arguably the most important one in the organization, and if it doesn't work, the rest of the organization feels it. It behooves you to ensure that you are working with the right strategic partner for the sake of your sanity and for the success of the organization. The first step to a successful EA-Executive partnership is making sure the time you will invest in each other will be time well spent. If you are not the right match, regardless of the strategies you implement, you will fail to build a fulfilling strategic partnership.

ACHIEVE MORE TOGETHER

- Are you working with the right strategic partner?
- If you suspect there may be a misalignment, have a conversation. Is the relationship repairable? Have you discussed how you can work together better?
- Do either of you need to change your communication style or increase your leadership skills?
- Leaders, do you have the right person but in the wrong seat in the organization?
- If you are working with the right strategic partner, congrats! How can you continue to challenge each other to grow in each of your roles?

WHEN THE ASSISTANT NEEDS AN ASSISTANT

These days, people wear "busy" like a badge of honor. Most people have too much on their plate. This includes Executive Assistants perhaps more than anyone, particularly in a startup. EAs handle everything from phone calls and emails to public relations, social media, contracts, interviews, vendor relationships, and more. As leaders, we are responsible for keeping an eye on our team (even if that team is just you and your EA).

When Entrepreneurs and Executives work at the pace they do, really for any startup or fast-growing company, they have to keep an eye out for employee burnout. Leaders must help manage their employees' energy, their workloads, and what they are focused on. We must pay attention to when they need a break and need some rest and recovery time. It's not as simple as time "on" and time "off," though. Most members of my team, myself included, would rather be working than doing pretty much anything else. Who am I to tell them not to work if they want to?

FOR BURNOUT

,t we do need to watch out for is real burnout. Burnout is
as the mental or physical collapse caused by overwork or
Rest, recovery time, and self-care strategies are critical to
avoid this. Taking time to unplug, exercise, get outside, or watch
a *Suits* marathon all have their time and place.

Burnout doesn't happen from the number of hours worked or
even from the intensity of the work. Burnout happens for several
main reasons:

1. You are not growing.
2. You are out of alignment with your natural behavior.
3. You are not having success for an extended period of time.

So how do you help your team avoid burnout?

UNDERSTAND YOUR TEAM MEMBERS' GOALS

First, make sure you have a clear understanding of your direct
reports' goals, personally and professionally. Are you meeting
with your team members regularly? Are you encouraging them
to take on new projects? Do you truly understand what motivates
them? If your team members start to feel stagnant or feel there
is no room for them to grow at your company, the work they do
tends to become less engaging and can lead to stress, which leads
to burnout. Make sure you have a clear growth plan for each of
the positions in your company, and communicate that often. Not
everyone will take you up on it. But knowing that growth is available is often enough.

UNDERSTAND YOUR TEAM MEMBERS' NATURAL BEHAVIOR

Do you understand the natural behavior of each of your team members? Do you know how they respond to stress? Do you know what work environments they thrive in? Do you understand their communication styles? If you answered no to even one of these questions, it's time to do a deep dive into your team members' personalities and behaviors. Once you have a clear understanding of their behaviors, you've got to ask yourself if they are in the right position in your company to achieve success.

For example, if you have a "High i" personality (refer to the DiSC profile) who is in a data entry position, with limited people contact, that is a complete mismatch. Now, any intelligent individual can learn and perform a job. But they are not going to be fulfilled, and they are likely going to be stressed each day operating outside of their natural behavior. And if that goes on for too long, it can lead to burnout. Again, burnout isn't just about the number of hours worked, but it also stems from time spent on projects, tasks, or a job that is not the right fit.

Matching natural behavioral styles with the behavior needed to thrive in a position is the cornerstone of our hiring practice. However, occasionally mismatches occur. If you know your team, you can spot this and avoid burnout by shifting staff or tweaking job descriptions. In my opinion, the fastest road to burnout is if someone is in a company that they love but a role that leaves them unfulfilled. If your team isn't aligned with the mission or vision of the company or their leader, then burnout will happen much, much faster. Make sure people are aligned not only with the right position for their behavior but also with where you and the company are going.

CREATE MINI VICTORIES

Burnout also occurs when an individual is failing over and over and over again. Okay, yes, I am a proponent of failure and failing forward. But there comes a point where a team member can just be banging their head against the wall, trying to get through, and nothing seems to be working. Failure like this, for a long time, with no clear wins, can be exhausting and deflating and can cause burnout.

This is where you need to step in. Does your employee need to step back and take a day off? Do they need some additional training? Do they need to be taken off the project or have someone else come in to help? Is it simply too much work for one person? Does your employee have the skills to accomplish what you are asking of them? Do they need help reprioritizing or chunking down the project into bite-size pieces so that they can accomplish one small part, have a victory, and then build upon that? Going too long without any success, no matter how small, is discouraging and stressful, which leads to burnout. Help your team members get wins that they can build on.

KEEP YOUR HEAD UP

Burnout can happen to the best of us. As a leader, it is your responsibility to keep an eye on your team, watch for signs of burnout, and mitigate it as much as possible. Employee burnout can have massive financial repercussions for your company in the form of costly mistakes, missed opportunities, or having a skilled employee leave. For your team members, the cost could be even greater, with effects on their mental and physical health. When your team members have their heads down, getting stuff done, it's your job to keep your head up and scan the room and the company for signs of burnout so you can redirect focus for the good of your team and your company.

If your business is growing rapidly or becoming more and more complex, what one person was able to handle at one point may no longer be possible. If your Executive Assistant is one of your first hires, which it will be for many Entrepreneurs, then at some point your assistant is going to need an assistant.

That's what happened to Hallie several years ago. Take a listen to her story. It took us a couple of tries to get it right, but it was worth it!

HALLIE NARRATES: ASKING FOR HELP

So how do you tell your boss when you simply have too much to do? No one wants to appear lazy, uncommitted, incompetent, or like they're not a team player. How can you protect your image as a hardworking, dedicated professional while essentially calling "uncle"? Well, it's not easy, but as with most difficult things, it starts with a conversation.

Look, your boss isn't completely unaware of the fact that you may have made a few mistakes lately (and you never make mistakes), you are working extremely long hours (not just once or twice a week but every day), and you no longer seem happy or fulfilled in your role (no matter how good you think you're faking it). These are some of the classic signs of burnout, and it's time to raise the white flag. This does not mean you have failed or that you are a failure! It simply means that the company is growing, and that's a good thing! You need help with your workload in order to continue to assist your Executive at the level that he expects from you and that you expect from yourself.

I've had two or three of these moments over the years working with Adam. I hate asking for help or admitting defeat (which is what it felt like when I could no longer handle the workload, no matter how many hours I worked). This happened several times because the company has grown tremendously in the past eleven years, with many iterations along the way.

The first time I made an Executive Assistant hire to replace myself in that capacity was about eight years ago. I had my hand in administration and operations not only for Adam but for three other companies. We hired an assistant to help split my workload, so then we had two of us with our hands in three companies. Not the most effective solution. Over the next couple of years, we went through several EAs in that role and ultimately decided to hire specific administrative and operational support for each organization rather than relying on one person with divided focus. That worked really well for the next couple of years. I was able to leverage some of my responsibilities while continuing to focus on my strengths as EA and Chief of Staff to Adam.

About five years ago, we went through more growing pains and hired a new assistant to help with my workload. I was able to leverage a lot of social media, marketing, and event coordination to that individual. Slowly, I was eliminating complete jobs from my list of responsibilities, and it felt great!

In mid-2017, it was no longer solely an issue of workload, but rather a combination of workload, feeling stagnant, and not being completely aligned in my position. You see, working so closely with Adam over the past eleven years gave me unique insight into various positions in our company, taught me a tremendous amount about leadership, and gave me the opportunity to really create a career that was the best fit for my strengths. Turns out, I am much better suited to being in a leadership position than being totally in the details all the time. I know we have talked about this before—yes, Executive Assistants are leaders too! However, with the size and the scope of our organization, it was becoming increasingly difficult to handle all the personal items and the day-to-day operational responsibilities as well as to fulfill the strategic, growth-oriented responsibilities that were part of my role.

Once we figured this out (I think it took us almost four years!), we decided to hire an Executive Assistant who would replace me in terms of managing Adam's day-to-day personal and business affairs and who would also help me with miscellaneous projects as they arose.

The assistant to the assistant can come in many different forms. You have to figure out what works for you. The assistant to the assistant could even be a completely new position. For example, perhaps your EA needs to leverage all bookkeeping and accounting tasks first, and after that she may look for someone to take over all marketing responsibilities. The next hire is going to be dependent on your Executive and the business. Choose wisely so that you truly get the assistance you need.

One other word of advice (clearly, speaking from experience here): speak up sooner rather than later! It will likely be an extensive interviewing and hiring process to find someone who can live up to your expectations, let alone the expectations of your Executive, who has been used to working with you, and only you, for many years. It could be six months or more before you find the right person. Furthermore, while unintentional, you may actually be slowing down the growth or efficiency of your organization by trying to do all the work yourself.

For Executives, hiring additional staff to assist their Executive Assistant may just be the best thing that happens for them and their business since they hired their Executive Assistant in the first place.

ACHIEVE MORE TOGETHER

- Have you checked yourself or your team members for burnout lately?
- What is the next logical position to hire to provide additional support and leverage on your team?
- Does your Force Multiplier need an assistant or some sort of additional support?
- Force Multipliers, do you need additional support in your role? Have you talked to your leader about it? Now's your chance to do so!

THE DIFFERENCE BETWEEN AN EXECUTIVE ASSISTANT AND A CHIEF OF STAFF

When the assistant needs an assistant, two roles can emerge—Executive Assistant and Chief of Staff—like they did at our company.

As the Chief of Staff role becomes more prominent in the corporate sector, many business leaders and Entrepreneurs want to know: what is the difference between an Executive Assistant and a Chief of Staff? Is it just semantics? What distinguishes these two roles? Both positions are often misunderstood, but there is one thing I know for sure: both positions are Force Multipliers.

EXECUTIVE ASSISTANTS AND CHIEFS OF STAFF

Through our continuous research on both the EA and Chief of Staff roles, patterns began to emerge. Yes, there is overlap between the two roles. Yes, a top EA may work on special projects in a strategic capacity as one CEO's Chief of Staff, while another EA may be more administrative and tactical. Yes, in some cases the titles are interchangeable. However, when both an EA and Chief of Staff exist in an organization, the roles are quite unique yet interdependent and offer two distinct career paths.

Currently, the most common way to define the two roles is this: Executive Assistants are tactical, and Chiefs of Staff are strategic. However, that is a gross oversimplification, and one we've used far too often in the past. But we're here to set the record straight. EAs are some of the most strategic individuals in an organization. Have you ever witnessed an Executive Assistant pull off a seemingly impossible trip, navigate the complexities of scheduling multiple Executives with competing demands, or save the day minutes before an event? Yeah. That's all strategy, planning, extreme resourcefulness, and yes, tactics, too. Conversely, Chiefs of Staff rely on both strategy and tactics daily—working on big-picture items and then breaking them down into actionable steps, communicating the vision, and holding various stakeholders accountable to the results.

I think a better differentiation between the two roles lies in time and overall responsibilities. How EAs and Chiefs of Staff go about getting the job done involves both strategy and tactics. They are simply working on different parts of one big, important, high-impact job.

EXECUTIVE ASSISTANTS LIVE IN THE NOW

Executive Assistants live in the now, or usually one week to thirty days out. Again, this doesn't mean they aren't planning for future events or travel or chipping away at longer-term projects. It simply means their work is driven by the demands of the day and week—meeting prep; handling phone calls, emails, and visitors; scheduling; answering questions that come into the Executive Office; keeping the CEO on track and on time; managing and organizing files and information; researching; preparing travel; etc.

A successful EA thrives in a supportive leadership role. She is organized and highly detail-oriented and enjoys handling administrative tasks. She is an exceptional communicator and a high performer and can handle a high volume of work with a sense of urgency without letting quality slip. An Executive Assistant prefers to handle short-term (though no less important) tasks one after the other and move on to the next.

CHIEFS OF STAFF LIVE IN THE FUTURE

Chiefs of Staff live in the future, or a minimum of ninety days out, though anywhere between ninety days and one year, and often beyond. They handle what they must in the moment, but much of their time is focused on longer-term planning and projects to ensure the growth of the organization and the success of the CEO. Their work is driven by the demands of the Founder's or CEO's long-term vision—interviewing for future leadership positions, creating a family office, writing a book, creating presentations or writing speeches to share the vision, meeting with potential business partners, refining recruiting and retention processes, establishing OKRs (objectives and key results), and more.

Just like an EA, a Chief of Staff thrives in a supportive leadership role. They prefer to be behind the scenes, holding the space for the CEO to express their genius and flow. A Chief of Staff prefers to dig into bigger, more complex issues. They enjoy working on big-picture items and are okay waiting to see the results of their work and initiatives. There is not much immediate satisfaction for a Chief of Staff!

The above just scratches the surface of both roles. Specific job descriptions are a bit harder to define, as they are dependent on the Executive, the organization, the industry, and more. Suffice it to say, they are both integral parts of an organization and key partners to a CEO's success.

WHY LEADERS NEED A CHIEF OF STAFF AND AN EXECUTIVE ASSISTANT

We know that the Executive Assistant and Chief of Staff positions are two distinct roles that both support the Executive. But is it really necessary for leaders to have both roles on their team? I think so.

I've had a Chief of Staff and an Executive Assistant for over five years now, and one of the most common questions I get is: "What do they do?" Well, you'd have to ask them; I'm not entirely sure. Really. That's the point, right? What I do know is that I am able to focus on my 20 percent because I have my Chief of Staff and my EA beside me.

Now, I didn't hire a Chief of Staff. As you know, my Chief of Staff, Hallie, started as my Executive Assistant over eleven years ago and grew into the position, taking on more and more projects and leading alongside me as my companies grew and became more complex, as we added new teams, new divisions, and new projects. About seven years ago, the workload was such that it necessitated our search for, and eventual hire of, an Executive Assistant.

WHAT DO THESE ROLES HAVE IN COMMON?

The Chief of Staff and the EA are both Force Multipliers. They take the Executive's vision and make sure it is carried out. They both lead and assist a CEO and typically only report to the Founder or another C-suite Executive. Strategy and tactics combined, they are the ultimate C-suite Dream Team. A great Chief of Staff and EA will work together to get things done before you even know you needed them.

With both a Chief of Staff and an EA on staff, an Executive can not only be extremely focused on just the most important issues each day (thanks to the support of their EA), but he also can be in two places at once (thanks to his Chief of Staff). Let me give you a couple of examples of how the Executive–Chief of Staff–Executive Assistant relationship works in my organization:

1. When I am on my one-to-one coaching calls each week (which my EA has scheduled and often rescheduled, and then prepared any documents or notes for me), my Chief of Staff is meeting with potential talent or future business partners for our company. My EA has ensured we are both in our meetings when we need to be and then asks us for feedback and follow-up items so that nothing is forgotten or missed.

2. When I'm hosting a full-day training seminar, my Executive Assistant plans and organizes the entire event, arrives early to set up, and ensures that the day goes smoothly, so all I have to do is show up and be totally present while teaching. My EA

also makes sure the attendees have everything they need and checks in with them during the breaks. Meanwhile, my Chief of Staff gives tours of the office to current and future business partners and makes connections with and for the attendees, makes notes on what content we should adjust, and scouts the room for talent.

Makes sense, doesn't it? Why wouldn't a leader want both a Chief of Staff and an EA on staff?

Now, I do want to be clear that not all Executives or companies need both an EA and a Chief of Staff. It really is dependent upon the size and scope of the organization, as well as the growth stage of the company. Don't get starry-eyed by the thought of all of this additional leverage if it doesn't make good financial sense for your business.

However, if you are an Executive with multiple divisions and complex business systems, an Entrepreneur with several companies and business ventures with multiple stakeholders, or a Founder in a high-growth startup, you likely need an Executive Assistant and a Chief of Staff. Your day will run more smoothly, you will be able to serve your company at a higher level, and you will be able to maximize your vision, reach more people, and ultimately grow and scale your company bigger and faster, all while maintaining your sanity (at home and at the office).

ACHIEVE MORE TOGETHER

- Do you need an Executive Assistant and Chief of Staff on your team? Why or why not?
- How would your organization benefit from having both roles?
- What potential issues could arise by having both an Executive Assistant and Chief of Staff working with you? Are those challenges you are willing to work through? Would the benefits outweigh any challenges?

NEVER STOP GROWING
AND LEADING

If you've been working with an Executive Assistant for at least three years, it's safe to say that you have found a good match and you want the partnership to keep growing. You really don't want a lot of turnover in the EA position. Years ago, a consultant told me and Hallie that the Executive Assistant position is a dead-end job. Sounds pretty terrible, but what he meant was that you want someone in that position working alongside you for a long time. Jack Welch's EA, Rosanne Badowski, worked with him for thirteen years at GE. When he retired from the company in 2001, she went with him to work on his next venture in Boston, and later in Florida. I guarantee both Jack and Rosanne grew exponentially in those years. Her title may not have changed, but she changed. They changed and grew together.

How do you create a partnership with your Executive Assistant like that of Jack and Rosanne?

KEEP WORKING TOGETHER

We're bringing it all the way back to the beginning. The same things that create a strong strategic partnership from the beginning will help the partnership thrive long term. When expectations change, communicate them. When life happens for either you or your EA, you may need to reset standards. Working through this together will be critical to a long and successful partnership.

Have each other's backs. It's your EA's job to take care of you. But to really make this relationship work, you've got to take care of your EA too. Do not let internal or external stakeholders take advantage of your EA. Cultivate trust and loyalty at every opportunity. Show each other respect publicly and privately. A little goes a long way.

PROVIDE OPPORTUNITIES FOR GROWTH

If you hired a talented EA, she will not be content to rest on her laurels. Whether it's providing her a fitness trainer, a life coach, or the opportunity to attend national conferences, give her the opportunity to learn and grow. Whatever she learns will only strengthen the partnership in the future.

Hand in hand with training and coaching is allowing your EA to take on new projects and responsibilities. Perhaps she heads up your events committee, takes over your social media marketing, or sets up a nonprofit for you. In order for your EA to remain engaged and growing, she will need to keep learning and taking on increasingly challenging projects.

BE FLEXIBLE

You don't want to be micromanaged. You also work weird hours and often work from home. Why should your EA be any different? Your EA has your schedule and is intimately aware of the work that needs to get done for herself and for you. If she needs to work from home a few times a month or wants to meet a friend for lunch, let her. As long as the work is getting done, there should be no issues. Talented EAs need the freedom and flexibility to manage their work. They also need the latitude to make decisions and act. If you are micromanaging an EA's every move, why did you hire her in the first place?

MAINTAIN YOUR CONNECTION

As the years progress and you've been working with your EA for five, six, or seven years, you may start to feel like you don't need to meet with her as often, check in with her, or give her guidance and direction. Wrong. Remember how we discussed the need for top EAs to be aligned with strong leaders? That doesn't lessen with time. If anything, that need grows. If you are not communicating and connecting with your EA regularly, she may disengage from the partnership. An EA's success is so closely tied to her Executive's that without regular connection, she may start to flounder and feel underutilized and undervalued. There is a fine line between having freedom and feeling forsaken.

GROW TOGETHER

Make sure you are continuing to grow and lead yourself first. If you don't continue to increase your leadership lid, your Executive Assistant may outgrow you. Take classes, study new business models, or host a book club together. Invest into each other's growth, and you'll both continue to thrive.

OWN YOUR FORCE MULTIPLIER CAREER

Now, it's a beautiful thing when an Executive understands the importance of investing in their strategic business partner. The companies that invest in their employees are the companies that are going to build a stronger workforce, retain talent, build trust and loyalty with their team members, and ultimately succeed (arguably better and faster than their competitors).

Yet sometimes, no matter how strong your proposal is, your boss or organization will deny your request for professional development funds. So now what? Well, Hallie's going to answer that question.

HALLIE NARRATES: INVEST IN YOURSELF

So what do you do when you aren't getting the support you would like from your company?

Take control of your career and invest in yourself.

Don't let a small (or nonexistent) training or continuing education budget stop you. Your career is up to you.

Yes, I understand that in theory, the course you are looking to take has a direct impact on your current job—hence why your company *should* pay for it. But I think we need to look more long term. Will you be at your current job forever? Maybe. Maybe not. If it is a coaching program or training that will enhance your professional skills or help you level up as a leader, then regardless of who is footing the bill, isn't it worth it to take that class? By investing in yourself and your career development, you make yourself not only a more valuable employee but also a stronger candidate for opportunities in the future. If your current employer helps pay for that, amazing! And if they don't, don't let that stop you from taking control and owning your Force Multiplier career.

Here are some benefits to investing in your own career growth:

- It shows that you are committed to and have ownership over your own career. Your boss or company will respect your investment in yourself, and the next time you submit a proposal for professional development, they may look at it differently. Maybe you go in on the next training 50/50 and go from there.
- You will be able to take what you learned, implement it at the office, and share it with your boss (at no cost and no risk to them). Showing them the value will make the next ask more impactful.
- Your additional training and certifications could be a point of leverage in your next compensation review or during a future job offer negotiation.
- Career development courses offer great networking opportunities to help you perform better at your current position or to tap into when you're looking for your next career opportunity.
- Enhancing your skillset makes you a more valuable employee now and a stronger candidate in the future.

Invest in yourself on a budget.

If you are serious about growing your career, then do not let a no from your boss or HR stand in your way. There are so many amazing training opportunities out there for Executive Assistants, Chiefs of Staff, and Personal Assistants—many of which are free or low cost. Online forums, podcasts, books, LinkedIn articles, and blogs are all easy ways to enhance your knowledge and skills. There are several Executive Assistant platforms that offer free trainings. And with the move to online events, the opportunities are endless for full-day summits, certification programs, coaching, and more. Bottom line: if you are truly committed to growing your career, you will find a way.

There is only one you. You are your greatest asset. Investing in yourself is the best investment you can make. Investing in yourself will pay dividends over time (not just monetarily, but with your own personal growth, your relationships, and more). Whether it's an MBA, an immersive meditation experience, a course to level up your leadership at work, or a fitness class, learning, growing, and creating the best version of yourself is always a good investment.

I will leave you with this quote:

"Investing in yourself is the best investment you will ever make. It will not only improve your life, it will improve the lives of those around you."
—ROBIN SHARMA

And that is just what you and your leader want to do in order to build a lasting and successful strategic partnership, as well as create a thriving business and fulfilling career.

ACHIEVE MORE TOGETHER

- If you have been working together for three or more years, set aside a few hours to revisit expectations, boundaries, schedules, priorities, and opportunities for growth. Make sure you are both still aligned on your goals and vision.
- What is the next area of opportunity for growth for you and your Force Multiplier?
- At the beginning of the year (or right now!), work together to determine a training budget. Bonus points for identifying specific courses, coaching, or conferences that your Force Multiplier will join throughout the year. Better yet, attend them together!
- What can you do to invest into yourself over the next thirty days?

CONCLUSION

WHAT'S NEXT?

What's next? This is a question that Hallie and I ask each other frequently. For such a simple question, it carries limitless opportunity, and we're taking full advantage of all that potential.

Listen, at the end of the day, what is life all about? I believe it's about coming into any relationship or partnership as a fully present and authentic being. And when each party does this, you're able to continue to work on the partnership by working on yourself. That's the real personal and spiritual growth that we get to experience while operating in the business world.

And yes, it's about business too! We already have several new projects underway, including three new books, hosting Project | U *Unbound* (a groundbreaking event for a small group of business leaders focused on spiritual growth), launching a SaaS company, and hiring additional leaders for my companies, and that's just in the next twelve to eighteen months! Regardless of where the future takes us, we are committed to continuing the partnership and pushing each other to grow.

You now have the playbook for building your own powerful strategic partnership. Go out there and use these best practices and resources for whatever is next for you!

Remember, beside every leader is a talented Force Multiplier. Beside every Force Multiplier is a visionary leader. Founders and Force Multipliers take turns leading the way, and by doing so, they achieve more together. And yes, so can you!

RESOURCES

BOOK BONUSES

Don't let your learning, growing, and leading stop when you finish this book! We have several resources for you to download, including the Weekly Execution Plan, the User's Manual, and Force Multiplier Job Descriptions. In addition, we've compiled all the Achieve More Together questions and action items into one easy-to-reference guide.

Access the book bonuses at:

founderandforcemultiplier.com/bookbonuses

THE INNER CIRCLE

The Inner Circle is a weekly newsletter designed to help Founders and Force Multipliers work smarter, lead stronger, live better, and grow faster. Sign up to receive event reminders, new blog posts, Hallie's top five picks of the week, and our most valuable content to help you grow your business, your career, and your strategic partnership.

Subscribe to *The Inner Circle* at:

founderandforcemultiplier.com/innercircle

TRAINING AND EVENTS

We are committed to helping you level up your career and strategic partnership through free online training and other events. We look forward to seeing you at a future event!

Check out our upcoming trainings and events at:

founderandforcemultiplier.com/events

YOUR FUTURE SELF

You can be anywhere you want to be in three years. Your Future Self is your North Star, your navigation that will guide you toward the life you're dreaming about. Use our online tool and fill in your three-year goals for each of the six (Professional, Financial, Physical, Social, Family, Spiritual) different areas of your life. Write in the present tense as if you've already accomplished them. It's about creating the life you want. This is not a time to think small or put limits on yourself. The more you focus on Your Future Self, the more real that version of you becomes. If you read it daily, it will only be a matter of time before you are living the life you imagined.

Once complete, we will email Your Future Self daily so you can read it while you're checking your emails. Simple. This is your guide for where you are going and who you are going to become.

adamhergenrother.com/future

Made in the USA
Monee, IL
14 December 2022

21674710R00154